Kaitlin Calogera | Rebecca Grawl

111 Places
in Women's History
in Washington
That You
Must Not Miss

Photographs by Cynthia Schiavetto Staliunas

emons:

For our foremothers and for our future

Did you enjoy this guidebook? Would you like to see more?
Join us in uncovering new places around the world on:
www.111places.com

Foreword

We were professional tour guides long before we became authors. Storytelling is our strength, and exploring places is our passion. But as our careers and perspectives grew, we felt compelled to reframe the narrative. In order to bring history forward, women deserved better representation in public spaces.

An idea became a business in 2018 when Kaitlin founded A Tour Of Her Own (TOHO), the first tourism company in Washington, DC to focus exclusively on women's history. The vision to create a sustainable culture of women's tourism was manifested into reality with genuine support from Rebecca, whose knowledge and commitment helped propel the business forward significantly.

Just as we hit momentum in March 2020, the tourism industry was instantly devastated by COVID-19. During a time of prohibited travel, we pivoted to transfer tourism from the streets of DC onto the pages of this book; *111 Places* was our pandemic project. We certainly encountered obstacles trying to navigate a city recovering from unprecedented events, but, despite six feet of social distancing, we ultimately discovered connection. Our stories of people and places often intersected, and when pieced together, they formed a more comprehensive narrative.

The demands of modern women were heightening in real time, but just as our foremothers, they triumphed to emerge as essential healers in our collective wellbeing. Grateful for our health and mindful of this historic moment, we wanted to offer our own contributions. With intention, we designed a guidebook that would promote and rebuild the tourism and hospitality industries. With pride, we showcased sites that would express the character and legacy of our capital city. With respect, we wrote stories that would honor women who broke ceilings and crawled on glass for us. It is our pleasure to share with you our deep appreciation for women's history in Washington, DC.

111 Places

1 AKA Sisterhood Mural
Kamala Harris, Madam Vice President

The date was January 20th, 2021, and Americans were preparing for the inauguration of the first woman to be elected as vice president. Ladies across the country laced up their Converse shoes and donned beautiful pearl necklaces in celebration of Kamala Harris. "Chucks" sneakers are a playful fashion preference for Madam Vice President, but the pearls are a symbolic jewelry of her sorority.

Alpha Kappa Alpha (AKA) was founded in 1908 at DC's Howard University, a prestigious historically Black college, where Harris graduated from in 1986. The everlasting connection between all Howard alumni is quite remarkable, but the members of AKA form a bond stronger than friendship; they are a sisterhood. When Kamala Harris was sworn into office, she too was wearing her pearl necklace and representing not only the people of the United States, but also her nearly 300,000 sisters from Alpha Kappa Alpha (see ch. 89).

The *Sisterhood* mural is located on the back wall of the Xi Omega Chapter building and was painted by artists Rose Jaffe and Kate DeCiccio. It features several of the sorority's founders, who are often referred to as "Twenty Pearls." Their portraiture shows them wearing their necklaces and surrounded by bold words – "Service," "Education," "Justice," and "Legacy." Any trained eye will notice the more intricate representation of the sorority; the pink tea rose, their official flower, and the official AKA symbol and magazine name, *Ivy Leaf*. Notable members of Alpha Kappa Alpha include singer Marian Anderson, tennis star Althea Gibson, and astronaut Mae Jemison.

Another notable member is Maya Angelou (see ch. 63), whose presence was on stage with Kamala Harris on January 20th when Amanda Gorman delivered her poem, "The Hill We Climb." As the youngest poet to ever perform at an inauguration, Gorman wore a caged bird ring, gifted to her by Oprah Winfrey in honor of Maya Angelou's memoir, I Know Why The Caged Bird Sings.

Address 4411 14th Street NW, Washington, DC 20011, www.muralsdcproject.com/mural/ sisterhood | Getting there Metro to Columbia Heights (Yellow and Green Line); bus 54 to 14th & Webster Streets NW | Hours Unrestricted | Tip Artists Jaffe and DeCiccio also collaborated on a mural titled *Cup Of Community* near the restaurant Soup Up, owned by Donna Henry (709 Kennedy Street NW, www.petworthnews.org/blog/soupup-kennedy).

2 Alethia Tanner Park

A self-emancipated woman

"There is a belief that you die twice: once when your body physically dies, and a second time when people stop saying your name." These were the words first said by Susan Cook when she presented her testimony in front of the DC City Council. As a direct descendant of Alethia Browning Tanner, Cook went on to acknowledge Tanner's courageous life as an enslaved woman who bought her own freedom, in hopes that DC's next park would be named in honor of her ancestor.

The council approved, and so did the community. Residents of the Eckington neighborhood were offered four name options for the park. Nearly 2,000 votes were cast online and by mail, and the results proved overwhelming support for Tanner Park, receiving more than 65% of the votes. This new public space now serves the community and stands as a memorial to a local hidden figure known as "Lethe."

Tanner was born on a plantation in Prince George's County, Maryland in the late 1780s. Historical records indicate that she crossed paths with Thomas Jefferson at various times, but her story, nevertheless, is anchored in her freedom. Despite not knowing how to read or write, she had become a successful entrepreneur by growing fruits and vegetables and selling them at the market in President's Park (currently Lafayette Square). She earned $1400 and paid to emancipate herself in 1810.

She built a life in the District that supported the prosperity of her community. Tanner purchased the freedom of 19 family members, funded a school for free Black students, and co-founded the oldest Black church in the District's original 100 square miles. She would also earn a reputation as "the mother of the African Methodist Episcopal Church."

Susan Cook told the City Council that day, "Alethia Tanner is much more than a history lesson. My hope is this park will spark an interest in her life by those who walk, run, and play there."

Address 227 Harry Thomas Way NE, Washington, DC 20002, www.nomaparks.org/
nomagreen | Getting there Metro to NoMa-Gallaudet (Red Line); bus P6 to 3rd Street
& Randolph Place NE | Hours Daily 7am–9pm | Tip Tanner's descendant Peter D.
Cook designed the Watha T. Daniel/Shaw Neighborhood Library (1630 7th Street NW,
www.dclibrary.org).

3 Alice Roosevelt's House
The other Washington Monument

The first child of Theodore and Alice Roosevelt, little Alice lost her mother and her paternal grandmother during the first 48 hours of her life. Her father, wracked with grief, left her to be cared for by her aunt and called her Baby Lee.

At the age of 17, Alice became an instant celebrity, dubbed Princess Alice by the press when her father became president in 1901. Her unconventional behavior, like carrying a green garter snake named Emily Spinach in her purse, gained attention from the press. She often clashed with her father, as they both loved to be the center of attention. Of her rambunctious nature, such as sliding down the White House stairways and smoking cigarettes on the roof, President Roosevelt quipped, "I can do one of two things, I can be President of the United States or I can control Alice Roosevelt. I cannot possibly do both."

Alice married a politician, Nicholas Longworth III, in 1906, despite the fact that he was a noted playboy and 14 years her senior. They purchased their home at 2009 Massachusetts Avenue NW, now the Washington Legal Foundation headquarters, and made it the center of DC political and social life. Alice's wicked sense of humor often led to scandal, and surprises were often on the menu.

Alice and Nicholas were both rumored to have carried on numerous affairs. DC society openly acknowledged Alice's dalliance with Senator William Borah. She had one child at age 41, and she joked that she wanted to name her Deborah (as in "de Borah") instead of Paulina. Alice's friends referred to Paulina as "Aurora Borah Alice."

Remaining in her Dupont Circle home, Alice continued to stay connected to politics, earning herself the moniker, "The Other Washington Monument." She outlived her husband and daughter and became the custodian of her granddaughter, Joanna, with whom she remained close until her death in 1980 at the age of 96.

Address 2009 Massachusetts Avenue NW, Washington, DC 20036, www.dcwritershomes.
wdchumanities.org/alice-roosevelt-longworth | Getting there Metro to Dupont Circle (Red
Line); bus N6 to Massachusetts Avenue NW & 20th Street NW | Hours Viewable from
the outside only | Tip Head over to Shop Made in DC for products made by local artisans.
Founded by Stacey Price, the store showcases the creative side of DC, from art and apparel
to hot sauce and beauty products (1710 Connecticut Avenue NW, www.shopmadeindc.com).

4 Alice's Artistic Retreat

Alice Pike Barney, a creative New Woman

Along Sheridan Circle, in the heart of Embassy Row, stands a 1902 mansion designed by Waddy Wood for Alice Pike Barney. The mansion would become the Alice Pike Barney Studio House, part of the Smithsonian Institute until it was sold in 1999. Today, it hosts the Embassy of Latvia.

Alice Pike was born in Ohio and inherited a passion for the arts from her distiller father. She pursued singing and piano before turning her attention to painting. At age 17, she shockingly became engaged to 33-year-old explorer Henry Morton Stanley. But when Stanley went on a journey to Africa on *The Lady Alice* – a boat named for his intended – Alice ended up marrying another man named Albert Barney.

Alice had been keen to continue her artistic studies after marriage, but Albert wanted no such thing. So she tried to ignore her artistic passions – until a chance encounter with Oscar Wilde in 1882 convinced her to pursue her art, regardless of her husband's wishes.

Alice embraced her role as a "New Woman." She traveled extensively through Europe with her daughters, taking art classes and joining the salon set. She had her daughters educated at a feminist boarding school in France, and they grew up to be as free-spirited as Alice. When her daughter Natalie published a book of poems, Alice provided the illustrations, unaware that the poems were of a sapphic nature, and the women she had painted were her daughter's lovers. When news of the scandal reached DC, Albert went to Europe, destroyed copies of the book, and brought his wife home.

Albert died in 1902, just as Alice finished work on her new mansion. She would use the mansion as her base of artistic operations, hosting parties, salons, artists, and theater groups, and frequently showcased her own work, a legacy her daughters continued after her death. You can see many of Alice's paintings in the Smithsonian American Art Museum today.

STUDIO HOUSE
In Memory of
ALICE PIKE BARNEY
ARTIST · CIVIC LEADER
PHILANTHROPIST

Given to the
SMITHSONIAN INSTITUTION
by her daughters
· 1960 ·

Address 2306 Massachusetts Avenue NW, Washington, DC 20008, www.siarchives.si.edu/blog/alice-pike-barney-studio-house | Getting there Metro to Dupont Circle (Red Line); bus N6 to Sheridan Circle & Massachusetts Avenue NW | Hours Viewable from the outside only | Tip Walk over to Hank's Oyster Bar's Dupont Circle location for oysters and crab cakes. Chef and restaurateur Jamie Leeds named the signature restaurant for her father (1624 Q Street NW, www.hanksoysterbar.com/dupont-circle-menu).

5 Alma Thomas House

White House art inspired by a tree in Logan Circle

First Lady Michelle Obama stood at a podium in April 2015 to deliver opening remarks at the inauguration of the Whitney Museum of American Art's new location in New York City. Her invitation to the ceremony was a testament to her support for the arts and humanities, a commitment that the Obama administration exemplified just two months earlier with a historic contribution to the White House: a painting by Alma Thomas.

The public tour of the president's house became more colorful and more representative of the American people when the painting was added to the Old Family Dining Room. This moment marked Thomas' legacy as the first African American woman to have her art featured in the White House. The piece from 1966 is titled *Resurrection*, and the inspiration for it came from the house where Thomas lived since she was a teenager.

Thomas spent nearly four decades as a professional art teacher at Shaw Junior High School. Shortly into her retirement, she suffered an arthritic attack that limited her mobility, and she would continue her art career from her living room. It was here that she recalls sitting on a red chair, admiring the holly tree outside, and recognizing the beautiful patterns and bright colors that shone through the windowpane. "That tree changed my whole career, my whole way of thinking," she said.

Half a century later, the view Alma Thomas saw from her living room would hang in the White House, just one mile from her own house that is now marked with a historical plaque.

Her career would peak in 1972 when she was honored with a retrospective exhibit at the Corcoran Gallery of Art in conjunction with Howard University, where she was the first to graduate from their fine arts program. That same year, at the age of 80, Alma Thomas would become the first African American woman to have a solo exhibit at the Whitney Museum of American Art.

Address 1530 15th Street NW, Washington, DC 20005, historicsites.dcpreservation.org/items/show/596 | Getting there Metro to McPherson Square (Blue, Orange, and Silver Line); bus 52 to 14th Street NW & Rhode Island Avenue NW; DC Circulator to 14th & P Streets NW | Hours Viewable from the outside only | Tip Visit the Smithsonian American Art Museum to view *The Eclipse*, an Alma Thomas painting similar to *Resurrection* (8th & G Streets NW, www.americanart.si.edu/artwork/eclipse-24007).

6 American Veterans Disabled for Life Memorial

She served and sacrificed

Close your eyes and think of all the veterans who have served. Picture them in uniforms, saluting the nation. How do these veterans look?

Preconceptions about gender is just one of the struggles that women in the military have to confront, often having to validate their identity while simultaneously resisting stereotypes perpetuated in a patriarchal society. For women veterans with disabilities, the experience is multiplied. Not only are they at risk to suffer physical disabilities during their service but they also report the long-term mental health impact from Military Sexual Trauma (MST). While some wounded women navigate through their hardships in private, others have embraced the public as part of the healing process.

One notable woman is Senator Ladda Tammy Duckworth, an Iraq War Veteran and the first woman with a disability elected to Congress. As the daughter of a Marine who struggled to transition into civilian life, she had a desire to serve her country and make change from an early age. After earning her Master of Arts from George Washington University in 1992, she returned to deliver the 2017 commencement speech on the National Mall.

She referred to the day her helicopter was hit as her "Alive Day" and noted how she was grateful to be saved by her crew. "I survived to serve my nation again," Duckworth said. "Maybe I was done serving in combat, but I could see the next step in my life's path because it meant that I could serve my fellow veterans. After I got out of Walter Reed, I went to the VA, I ran for Congress and then I won my seat in the Senate."

The American Veterans Disabled for Life Memorial honors all who have sacrificed. Women included in our collective memory are illustrated by silhouettes and images.

Address 150 Washington Avenue SW, Washington, DC 20024, +1 (877) 426-2838, www.avdlm.org | Getting there Metro to Federal Center SW (Orange and Silver Line); bus 30N, 30S, 32, 36 to Independence Avenue & First Street SW | Hours Unrestricted | Tip Gail Cobb Way is named in memory of the country's first Black female police officer killed in the line of duty, a Washingtonian whose parents live on this corner (300 block of 14th Place NW, www.mpdc.dc.gov/page/memory-officer-gail-cobb).

7 — Anderson House

Isabel Weld Perkins, a jet-setting art patron

Completed in 1905, Anderson House was once heralded as "a Florentine villa in the midst of American independence." The mansion was a winter residence for diplomat Larz Anderson and his wife, Isabel Weld Perkins. For more than 30 years, it served as the backdrop for their society galas and massive collection of arts and antiques.

Larz Anderson married up when he joined lives with Isabel Weld Perkins. A Boston heiress, Perkins had ancestral ties all the way back to the Massachusetts Bay Colony and an inheritance rumored to be worth at least $5 million. At the age of 19, Perkins met Anderson in Rome, where he was posted as secretary of the US Embassy. They married two years later.

Isabel took advantage of her husband's diplomatic career to travel extensively and build a stunning collection of art and furniture. Not content to simply luxuriate in a life of leisure, Isabel turned her attention to writing. She wrote about American history and her family's role in it, travelogues about the countries and cultures she discovered as an ambassador's wife, poetry, children's stories, and plays.

During World War I, Perkins volunteered with the Red Cross in DC before heading to France and Belgium to care for the sick and wounded. When she returned to DC in 1918, she cared for those impacted by Spanish flu. She was ultimately awarded the Red Cross Service Medal, the French *Croix de Guerre*, and the Medal of Elisabeth of Belgium for her nursing contributions.

The Andersons had no children, so when Larz passed away in 1937, Isabel was responsible for preserving their legacy. She personally oversaw the donation of the Anderson House mansion to the Society of the Cincinnati, of which Larz was a member. It now serves as the society's national headquarters, and it hosts a public museum that documents the American Revolution and showcases the Andersons' extensive collections.

Address 2118 Massachusetts Avenue, Washington, DC 20008, +1 (202) 785-2040, www.societyofthecincinnati.org/visit/info | **Getting there** Metro to Dupont Circle (Red Line); bus N6 to Massachusetts and Florida Avenues NW | **Hours** Tue – Sat 10am – 4pm, Sun noon – 4pm | **Tip** Umber Ahmad grew up traveling the world but always kept her native Pakistani flavors close to her heart. In 2014, she founded Mah Ze Dahr Bakery, where visitors can experience the world through food (1201 Half Street SE, Suite 105, www.mahzedahrbakery.com).

8__Anna J. Cooper House
The only woman quoted in the US passport

Collecting international stamps in a passport is a rite of passage for many adventurous travelers, but the journey of Dr. Anna Julia Cooper is marked in ink before that little blue booklet ever leaves the country. She has the unique honor of being the only woman quoted in the United States passport. The excerpt reads, "The cause of freedom is not the case of a race or a sect or a party or a class – it is the cause of humankind, the very birthright of humanity."

Her life was defined by mobility. Born the daughter of an enslaved woman, Anna Julia Cooper would become a world traveler and an accomplished educator. Widowed after just two years of marriage, Cooper embraced her life as a public figure and delivered human rights speeches in London and at the Chicago World's Fair. She would travel to Paris, France to enroll as a student in the prestigious Sorbonne University, where, at the age of 66, she became the fourth Black woman in the United States to earn a Ph.D.

There's no question why the legacy of this worldly woman is stamped in the United States passport, but her story is also rooted in the neighborhoods of Washington, DC. Anna Julia Cooper shaped the culture of education to benefit the city's most underserved residents. She earned the role of principal at the Preparatory High School for Colored Youth. In the latter part of her life, she would go on to serve as president of Frelinghuysen University, a night school for working-class adults.

Dr. Cooper lived in this home for nearly 50 years before dying at the age of 105 in 1964, just months before the Civil Rights Act would be signed into law. Her house and the surrounding neighborhood of LeDroit Park were preserved by two women, Theresa Brown and Lauretta Jackson. The home's porch, admired by many for its elegance, once served as a graduation stage for the night students whom Dr. Anna Julia Cooper taught just inside her home.

Address 201 T Street NW, Washington, DC 20001, www.dcwritershomes.wdchumanities.org/anna-julia-cooper | Getting there Metro to Shaw-Howard University (Green and Yellow Line); bus 90, 92, 96, X3 to Florida Avenue NW & 6th Street NW | Hours Viewable from the outside only | Tip Admire a nearby mural, painted by 14 international female artists who collaborated in celebration of Women's History Month. Look for messages like, "Tell Your Her Story," and "Votes for Women" (73 Florida Avenue NW, www.albuscav.us/womenhistory.html).

9 Anne Royall's Grave
The first female congressional correspondent

Congressional Cemetery, officially the Washington Parish Burial Ground, is the only American "cemetery of national memory" founded before the Civil War. Established in 1807, the over 65,000 individuals honored here represent some of the best and brightest of this nation – and at least one very eccentric woman.

Anne Royall was born in 1769 and learned to read and write at a young age, a rarity for women in that era. She moved to present-day West Virginia to work for William Royall, whom she married in 1797. William introduced her to philosophy and freemasonry, and he encouraged her independence. When he died in 1812, leaving Anne with no children and a will that was nullified, she was penniless and had to forge her own path.

For six years, Royall traveled extensively across the United States, supporting herself with her writing and eventually publishing a nine-volume set of her adventures. *Sketches of History, Life, and Manners in the United States* (1826) thoroughly documented politics, education, religion, and vice across the country, incorporating statistics about crops, population, and trade as well.

She would continue writing both fiction and non-fiction, and she launched a weekly newspaper, *Paul Pry*, followed by another paper, *The Huntress*. The papers were notable for their exposés on government corruption and scathing editorials. Because of her political coverage, she is credited as the first female congressional correspondent.

Her tone was often antagonistic, and she was once convicted as a "common scold." Though her tenacity would often be to her benefit. She was rumored to have been so insistent to interview John Quincy Adams that she sat on his clothes during one of his daily naked swims in the Potomac River and refused to move until he answered her questions. He did so, keeping only his head above the water and later described her as "the terror of politicians."

Address 1801 E Street SE, Washington, DC 20003, +1 (202) 543-0539, www.congressionalcemetery.org, staff@congressionalcemetery.org | Getting there Metro to Stadium-Armory (Blue, Orange, and Silver Line); bus B2 to Potomac Avenue & E Street SE. Gravesite is in Range 26, Site 194. | Hours Daily dawn – dusk | Tip A favorite shop in Hill East is Hill's Kitchen, where owner and Capitol Hill native Leah Daniels stocks the best kitchen supplies and goodies in a historic townhouse dating to 1884 (713 D Street SE, www.hillskitchen.com).

10 Asbury UMC DC

Emily and Mary Edmonson's faith and freedom

Asbury United Methodist Church (UMC) is the oldest Black Methodist church in the city, founded in 1836. In its current location since 1870, the church has been a cornerstone of the Black community. Notable members include Mary Church Terrell (see ch. 97), who used the church as a meeting place in the 1940s for an interracial coalition; Mary McLeod Bethune (see ch. 56), who petitioned Franklin D. Roosevelt to recognize the church's centennial in 1936; and two sisters, whose family helped to found the congregation and who would be part of a daring escape attempt.

On April 15, 1848, 77 enslaved people in DC slipped out into the night, heading for *The Pearl*, a small ship docked at the southwest waterfront wharf, in a quest for freedom. The voyage would sadly be a short one. The ship only managed to get 140 miles up the Potomac River before weather forced the vessel to drop anchor. By then, a steamer ship was on its way, carrying a mob of white men, who would force those aboard back into slavery.

Among those attempting escape was the Edmonson family, with two teenage sisters Emily and Mary. When an angry crowd taunted *The Pearl'* spassengers as they exited the ship, Emily shouted in defiance that they would do it all again. Emily and Mary were sold to a slave trading firm in Alexandria, Virginia for $750 each and sent to New Orleans. Fortunately, their father was able to raise over $2000 to purchase their freedom.

The sisters would become well known in the abolitionist movement. Harriet Beecher Stowe, author of *Uncle Tom's Cabin*, published a chapter on the sisters in her nonfiction account of slavery and paid for both of them to attend Oberlin College. Sadly, Mary died of tuberculosis at age 20, but Emily would return to DC, live near her friend Frederick Douglass in Anacostia, and later assist educator Myrtilla Miner in establishing the city's first high school for Black students.

Address 926 11th Street NW, Washington, DC 20001, +1 (202) 628-0009, www.asburyumcdc.org, asburymail@asburyumcdc.org | Getting there Metro to Metro Center (Blue, Orange, Red, and Silver Line); bus 64, G8 to 11th & K Streets NW | Hours See website and services | Tip Sip on something rare from Pearl Fine Tea, founded by Elise Scott in 2007. She became the first certified tea master in DC by the Specialty Tea Institute. Her tasty teas are stocked at a variety of local farmers' markets (www.pearlfineteas.com).

11 Beau Thai

Aschara Vigsittaboot's mom inspires a curry

When Aschara Vigsittaboot moved to the United States in 2001, she started out as a server and grew into an entrepreneur. She met a customer named Ralph Brabham, who would become her future business partner alongside Drew Porterfield, and together, the trifecta built an empire known as Beau Thai.

It's not hard to imagine what Vigsittaboot's experience was like leaving southern Thailand as an exchange student with AFS Intercultural Programs because a photo of her initial departure hangs inside the restaurant to depict her story. Fast forward several years, and the original Beau Thai has been rebranded BKK Cookshop – the Bangkok airport code.

Walking into the Shaw and Mount Pleasant establishments is like time-traveling to the past and getting a glimpse of Southeast Asia. The wall art pays homage to Aschara's family, with a special focus on her mother, Udom, who attended culinary school and taught her daughter everything she knows about cooking. Aschara recalled analyzing a plate of curry in the US and saying, "No, it's wrong." So she recreated the traditional Thai dish herself, perfected it from scratch, put it on the menu, and named it "Udom's Curry" in honor of her mother. The classic photos hanging at Beau Thai are matched with an edgy and modern vibe influenced by Brabham and Porterfield, a married couple, who infuse their North Carolina roots into the beverage list and brunch menu.

Vigsittaboot enjoys the four seasons of weather in Washington, DC, and she remembers seeing snow for the first time here. She not only opened a business here but became a respected member of the community. Beau Thai makes considerable donations in support of local organizations, like My Sister's Place and New Endeavors by Women. She also teaches cooking classes for locals to further her mission of "Making everybody in the community healthy in the way that they eat."

Address 3162 Mount Pleasant Street NW, Washington, DC 20010, +1 (202) 450-5317, www.beauthaidc.com, beauthaidc@gmail.com | Getting there Metro to Columbia Heights (Yellow and Green Line); bus H8 to Mount Pleasant & 17th Streets NW | Hours See website | Tip For more than 20 years, Dos Gringos' owner Alex Kramer has served tasty, affordable, non-processed food inspired by her New York roots and Salvadorian staff. Bring a book to read (maybe this one), as laptops are not allowed (3116 Mount Pleasant Street NW, www.dosgringosdc.com).

12 Belmont-Paul National Monument

Where women first fought

"We ratified the 19th Amendment. But the suffragists didn't stop there," said President Barack Obama at the ceremony designating the Belmont-Paul Women's Equality National Monument (2016)

Long adored as a place of local history, the former headquarters of the National Woman's Party (NWP) became a national monument during this ceremony. Here inside one of the oldest homes on Capitol Hill, you can explore the story of the hard-fought battle for equal rights for women in the rooms where it happened. Originally completed in 1800, the building was sold to Alice Paul and the NWP in 1929.

The NWP, founded by Paul in 1916 to shift the fight for women's suffrage to a constitutional amendment, had been the more militant wing of the suffrage movement, staging protests outside the White House and hunger strikes inside their jail cells. After the ratification of the 19th Amendment, Paul went back to school, earned three law degrees, and refocused the fight for equality through the law. In 1923, she drafted the Equal Rights Amendment and supported the legislation for the next 50 years. In 1943, in honor of her tireless work on the issue, the amendment was renamed in her honor. Spearheaded by Paul, the NWP continued its work for gender inclusion at the United Nations and equality in legislation such as the Civil Rights Act of 1964.

On display here is the NWP's robust collection of portraits and sculptures featuring pivotal female figures and leaders. But most importantly, look for the tools used by the female activists of this movement, including banners carried by the Silent Sentinels who protested outside the White House, as well as sashes, capes, and typewriters – all wielded with the single goal of women's equality at the ballot box and beyond.

Address 144 Constitution Avenue NE, Washington, DC 20002, +1 (202) 543-2240, www.nps.gov/bepa, bepa_info@nps.gov | Getting there Metro to Union Station (Red Line); bus 97 to Constitution Avenue NE & First Street NE | Hours Wed–Sun 9am–5pm | Tip Alice Paul tracked progress of the ratification of the Equal Rights Amendment on a charm bracelet, now displayed at the National Museum of American History – she added a charm for each state as it ratified, although she died in 1977, just three states short (1300 Constitution Avenue NW, www.americanhistory.si.edu).

13 Bené Millinery

Vanilla Beane, maker of crowns

In a town full of makers and creators, Vanilla Powell Beane is the original. The artist's custom-made hats add vibrant color and elegant design to community events in the District and beyond. From church services to wedding showers, wearing a hat from Bené Millinery & Bridal Supply is more than an accessory – it's an experience.

One of Beane's hats made an appearance at Barack Obama's Inauguration, donned by civil rights icon Dorothy Height (see ch. 20). The president later said, "We loved those hats that she wore like a crown." DC Mayor Muriel Bowser (see ch. 14) also wore one of the milliner's hats at a tea service honoring the local legend on her 100th birthday in 2019. At that event, the mayor declared September 13th "Vanilla Beane Day," in recognition of the centenarian's success as an entrepreneur. Bowser stated, "I think you have shown a lot of people that there is no sense of retiring."

Born in 1919, Beane was still working full-time hours and creating hand-sewn products one century later. Her experience in the industry dates back to the 1950s when she began working at the Washington Millinery & Supply Company. Initially, she was an elevator operator, but after experimenting with the fabrics during her down time there, she escalated into a job as a supply clerk. The owner of the millinery eventually retired and sold his supplies to Beane, who officially opened her Manor Park shop in 1979. It's been family-run ever since.

The self-taught seamstress has earned the reputation as "DC's Hat Lady." Her legacy is now enshrined in the Smithsonian, where a 3-D replica of her favorite green turban is part of the digital collection at the National Museum of African American History and Culture. Vanilla Powell Beane's signature power statement comes from her elementary school teacher: "Love Many. Trust Few. Learn to paddle your own canoe."

Address 6217 3rd Street NW, Washington, DC 20011, +1 (202) 722-0862, https://benemillinery.business.site | Getting there Metro to Takoma (Red Line); bus 62 to 5th & Sheridan Streets NW | Hours Mon–Sat noon–6pm | Tip Match a hat with an outfit from Beane's longtime neighbor, The Lovely Lady Boutique, owned by mother and daughter Ethel and Raynette Sanders (6213 3rd Street NW, www.lovelyladyboutique.net).

14 Black Lives Matter Plaza

#BreonnaTaylor: Say her name

Washingtonians woke up to a bold statement on Friday, June 5, 2020. Under the direction of District of Columbia Mayor Muriel Bowser, the phrase "Black Lives Matter" was painted on the road in extra large, bright yellow, capital letters. The message spanned across a considerable portion of 16th Street just north of the White House. The street corner just outside the historic Saint John's Church was renamed "Black Lives Matter Plaza," and a sacred space was reclaimed by the local community.

The street sign installed there on her birthday stands as a memorial to Breonna Taylor, a celebration of her life and a public reminder of her very tragic death that awoke the masses to chant her name in streets across the country. On the day the new sign was placed, Mayor Bowser tweeted these words, "Breonna Taylor, on your birthday, let us stand with determination. Determination to make America the land it ought to be." Taylor would have turned 27 years old on that day.

Like Mayor Muriel Bowser and Breonna Taylor, women's stories are rooted in the Black Lives Matter network. The movement was co-founded by three women: Alicia Garza, Patrisse Cullors, and Opal Tometi. They envisioned a movement that centered the leadership of women and other marginalized voices historically overlooked in civil rights movements. In the 1963 March on Washington for Jobs and Freedom, women were not included on the speaker schedule and were expected to participate in a separate march from the men. Women leaders in the movement like Dorothy Height (see ch. 20) and Daisy Bates were met with resistance when they fought for representation.

In a city abundant with monuments and memorials, Black Lives Matter Plaza has become one of the most sought-out places to visit today. The street sign is a symbol of a global movement started by women, led by women, and all too often in memory of women, including Breonna Taylor.

Address 1525 H Street NW, Washington, DC 20005, www.mayor.dc.gov | Getting there Metro to McPherson Square (Blue, Orange, and Silver Line); bus 30N, 30S, 32, 33, 36, 42, 43, S 2 to H Street & Madison Place NW | Hours Unrestricted | Tip On the Points of Light Volunteer Path look for a bronze sidewalk medallion recognizing Mary White Ovington and W. E. B. Du Bois as the co-founders of the NAACP (G Street NW between 13th & 14th, www.pointsoflight.org).

15 Café Mozart

Hildegard Fehr becomes an entrepreneur for $1.76

Walking into Café Mozart is like hopping a plane to Munich and arriving just in time for Oktoberfest. German culture takes over with the first step into this eclectic delicatessen shop. The shelves are stocked with Haribo gummy bears, Kinder chocolate, and Deutschland soccer gear. Authentic goods line both sides of the long aisle that eventually leads to the back restaurant and bar. With an ambiance that welcomes guests to lose track of time, it's the kind of place where a hearty *schnitzel* and a liter of *hefeweizen* lead to philosophical conversations with strangers at the bar.

As one of Washington, DC's oldest woman-owned restaurants, the glass display case showcasing a variety of traditional sausages holds an extra special meaning at Café Mozart. It started with a frustrated entrepreneur named Mary Faiss. In 1932, she opened the Annapolis Delicatessen on 11th Street NW, located inside the Manger Annapolis Hotel. One day in 1964, she had a moment of despair, when yet another shipment of products had been delayed. On a reactionary whim, she sold her delicatessen on the spot to Hildegard P. Fehr.

Hilde visited the deli that day prepared to purchase her regular order of three sausages but left with only two in her bag. She spent her remaining $1.76 on a down payment. Faiss told her, "You can have the store, I cannot take it anymore, give me a down payment, so I will not change my mind tomorrow."

Hildegard Fehr returned the next day with a full payment, and just a week later, the Austrian immigrant would become the owner of this District establishment. After a few location and name changes, it has stood the test of time just blocks away from the White House. In 1981, German Deli moved into the University of DC's cafeteria and became Café Mozart. Hilde has entrusted her business operations to the Ahmad family, who have been loyal employees to her for over 30 years.

Address 1331 H Street NW, Washington, DC 20005, +1 (202) 347-5732, www.cafemozart.com |
Getting there Metro to Metro Center (Orange, Silver, Blue, and Red Line); bus 52 to 14th &
I Streets; DC Circulator to K & 13th Streets | **Hours** See website | **Tip** After retiring as a first
grade reading teacher, Ann B. Friedman had an idea for a museum dedicated to language. Today,
Planet Word was created in the historic building of the Franklin School (925 13th Street NW,
www.planetwordmuseum.org).

16 Cherry Trees of DC

Eliza Scidmore, the woman behind the blossoms

Each spring, DC is transformed by a burst of pink and white when the Japanese cherry blossoms bloom. This event, usually lasting no more than 10 days, brings an estimated 1.5 million visitors to admire the more than 3,000 flowering trees in DC.

There is no marker or plaque commemorating Eliza Scidmore, the woman responsible for this annual blossoming. Eliza was a world traveler, geographer, photographer, and author, who became the first woman to sit on the board of the National Geographic Society. Her brother was a career diplomat to Asia, and Eliza was able to accompany him on many of his travels.

Frequent travel to Japan inspired Eliza to propose the idea in 1885 of planting Japanese cherry blossom trees in the nation's capital. Eliza wrote, "[T]he blooming cherry tree is the most ideally, wonderfully beautiful tree that nature has to show, and its short-lived glory makes the enjoyment keener and more poignant." Initial response was cold, but Eliza continued to advocate for the cause, proposing it every year to the Superintendent of Public Buildings and Grounds, as well as advocating to the press and writing letters to the White House. At every turn, the men in charge turned her down or ignored her entirely.

Finally, in 1909, Scidmore wrote to First Lady Helen Taft and found an ally in her quest. Taft had also traveled to Japan and seen the cherry blossoms firsthand and actively supported the cause. The project then moved forward rapidly. Scidmore proposed planting a majority of the trees on the newly reclaimed land of Potomac Park, which Taft endorsed. When a Japanese delegation learned of the plans, an offer was made to contribute the trees. On March 27, 1912, Helen Taft would plant the first cherry tree, and Scidmore was the only private citizen recorded in attendance. A plaque marks the spot where the first trees were planted, but Scidmore is not mentioned.

Address Independence Avenue SW, Washington, DC 20006, www.nps.gov/subjects/
cherryblossom/index.htm | Getting there Metro to Smithsonian (Blue, Orange, and Silver
Line); DC Circulator to MLK Memorial | Hours Unrestricted | Tip Eliza Scidmore's DC
residence (also once the home of author John Dos Passos) was located on M Street NW, in the
Dupont Circle neighborhood, and it's now the popular tapas bar Boqueria (1837 M Street NW,
www.boqueriarestaurant.com).

17 __ Contemplative Court
Frances Ellen Watkins Harper represents women

Frances Ellen Watkins Harper is the only woman represented inside the Contemplative Court at the National Museum of African American History and Culture. Designed to contrast with the rectangular layout of the museum, Contemplative Court features the circular Oculus that glistens like a glass curtain. This space serves as a meditative passage between the emotional historical exhibits below ground and the uplifting culture floors upstairs. The natural light is a release from dark exhibits, like that of Mamie Till and her son Emmett. The raining water provides purification and white noise for visitors to sit mindfully with their thoughts about the resilience of Black Americans throughout centuries of institutional racism.

Here you can reflect on the words of Frances Ellen Watkins Harper, one of the most impactful voices of the 19th century. The end of her poem, "Bury Me in a Free Land," spans one of the four walls: *I ask no monument, proud and high, To arrest the gaze of the passers-by; All that my yearning spirit craves, Is bury me not in a land of slaves.*

Harper was a free Black woman born in the slave state of Maryland. She traveled often as an activist involved in the abolition, suffrage, and temperance movements. Her career as a lecturer began with a poetry performance in 1853 that she delivered next to Mary Ann Shadd Cary (see ch. 61) in Philadelphia. She wrote several articles for Cary's newspaper *Provincial Freedom*. In an act of defiance the following year, Harper refused to forfeit her seat on a segregated horse-drawn trolley. She later formed a friendship with John Brown, leader of the Harper's Ferry raid, and spent two weeks with his wife Mary Anne Day Brown awaiting his execution.

Her same quote is highlighted in a documentary directed by Ava DuVernay. *August 28: A Day In The Life Of A People* plays on a continuous loop inside the museum. Watkins is quoted by actor Glynn Turman in a scene recognizing the Slavery Abolition Act of 1833.

I ASK NO MONUMENT, PROUD AND HIGH
TO ARREST THE GAZE OF THE PASSERS-BY;
ALL THAT MY YEARNING SPIRIT CRAVES,
IS BURY ME NOT IN A LAND OF SLAVES

FRANCES ELLEN WATKINS HARPER 1858

Address 1400 Constitution Avenue NW, Washington, DC 20560, +1 (844) 750 3012, www.nmaahc.si.edu, info@si.edu | **Getting there** Metro to Smithsonian (Blue, Silver, and Orange Line); DC Circulator to 15th Street & Madison Drive NW | **Hours** See website | **Tip** Enjoy a meal at RIS with Chef Lacoste, who sits on the advisory board for Smithsonian Food History programs and collections (2275 L Street NW, www.risdc.com).

18 — The Decatur House

Charlotte Dupuy sued for her freedom

This stately brick mansion has been home to a number of notable men, such as Stephen Decatur, Henry Clay, and Martin Van Buren. But it was also the home of an enslaved African American woman named Charlotte Dupuy, who used her time at the Decatur House to launch her legal fight for freedom.

Charlotte Dupuy was born into slavery in Maryland in the late 1780s. She was brought to Kentucky by a man named James Condon, who sold her to Henry Clay, a lawyer and politician, after she had married Aaron Dupuy, a man enslaved by Clay. When Clay came to DC in 1810, he brought Charlotte, Aaron, and their children with him to live and work at the Decatur House.

Living in the nation's capital inspired Charlotte to fight for her family's emancipation. When Henry Clay's term as secretary of state ended in 1829 and he made plans to return to Kentucky, Dupuy filed a petition for her family's freedom based on a promise of freedom that James Condon had made to her before he sold her to Clay. Dupuy would be allowed to stay in DC for 18 months while her case was examined in court. She stayed at the Decatur House, working for wages for Martin Van Buren, while her husband and children went back to Kentucky with Clay.

Henry Clay fought Dupuy in court, convinced that she was being coerced by his political enemies. Her freedom suit was denied, but Dupuy refused to return to Kentucky and was imprisoned before Clay had her transferred to New Orleans. Eleven years after the lawsuit, Clay granted Dupuy and her daughter freedom and her son four years later. Just before he died, Clay freed her husband in 1852.

Seventeen years before Dred Scott faced the Supreme Court, Dupuy's willingness to go to court and challenge a high-ranking politician publicly illustrates her bravery at a time when enslaved women had few avenues for emancipation.

Address 748 Jackson Place NW, Washington, DC 20006, +1 (202) 218-4333, www.whitehousehistory.org/plan-your-visit | Getting there Metro to McPherson Square (Blue, Orange, Red, and Silver Line); bus 30N, 30S, 32, 43, S 2 to H Street & Madison Place NW | Hours See website | Tip A mother's quest to find safe bath products inspired Leigh Byers to open Hunnybunny Boutique, a Black-owned business on Capitol Hill. The store is run by Nya and Zuri, her daughters, who test every product before it hits the shelves (311 8th Street NE, www.hunnybunny.boutique).

19 Dolley Madison House

The second-most-visited residence in Washington

When you think of the ideal First Lady – fashionable, kind, smart, tasteful, and graceful – it is impossible not to think of Dolley Madison. As our fourth First Lady, Dolley Payne Todd Madison established a standard that is still emulated 200 years later.

When Dolley married James Madison in 1794, she was a widow with a young son, looking for a new start. Though Madison was 17 years her senior and her polar opposite in personality, she said, "Our hearts understand each other." With a desire to bolster her husband's career when appointed Secretary of State, Dolley made herself the center of early DC society, assisting widower President Jefferson. When Madison became President, Dolley envisioned a grand celebration and presided over the very first inaugural ball in 1809.

She would be forced to flee the White House in 1814, when the city was attacked by the British Army, who set fire to the White House and other government buildings. She refused to leave without important government documents and insisted staff break the wooden frame of the portrait of George Washington so she could take the precious painting with her and not let it fall into enemy hands. Even when the Madisons could not return to the White House due to repairs after the attack, she entertained skillfully from their temporary home at the Octagon House (see ch. 71).

Dolley would return to DC in 1837 following the death of her husband and settle into the house along Lafayette Square. She continued entertaining and socializing, even hosting an annual New Year's Day reception with an open-door policy. Her home was said to be the second-most- visited residence in the city, after the White House itself. She died a beloved figure in 1849. As journalist Anne Royall (see ch. 9) wrote, "her power to please – the irresistible grace of her every movement – sheds such a charm over all she says and does that it is impossible not to admire her."

Address 811 Vermont Avenue NW, Washington, DC 20571, www.whitehousehistory.org/dolley-madison-house-on-lafayette-square | Getting there Metro to McPherson Square (Blue, Orange, and Silver Line); bus 30N, 30S, 32, 33, 36, 42, 43, S2 to H Street & Madison Place NW | Hours View from outside only | Tip Dolley Madison frequently served ice cream at the White House, helping to popularize the treat. Try modern interpretations on the classic dessert at Victoria Lai's Ice Cream Jubilee (1407 T Street NW, www.icecreamjubilee.com).

20 Dorothy Height Post Office

Godmother of Civil Rights

To be eulogized by a US president is an honor reserved for legends like Dorothy Irene Height. The final words commemorating her life were delivered by President Barack Obama at the Washington National Cathedral in 2010. She died at Howard University hospital but lived until the age of 98, having worked alongside some of the twentieth century's greatest leaders. She became known as the "Godmother of the Civil Rights Movement."

After decades of fighting for racial justice, Dr. Height was in attendance at the 2008 Presidential inauguration to witness the first Black person elected to the office. She would visit the White House 21 times as a friend of the administration, respected as a dignified elder with important stories to share. She was also a woman of action, involved with the YMCA and serving as president of the National Council of Negro Women (NCNW) for nearly four decades. She fundraised for NCNW projects like erecting a memorial for Mary McLeod Bethune (see ch. 56) and securing a new headquarters that would become the first Black-owned building in downtown Washington, DC.

Dorothy Height had a presence that radiated grace and class. She was admired for her bright colored outfits and matching accessories, but she was most recognized for her fashionable custom hats made by local DC milliner Vanilla Beane (see ch. 13).

Congresswoman Eleanor Holmes Norton introduced bill H. R. 6118 to add Dorothy Height's name officially to the post office at National Capitol Station, which shares space with the Smithsonian Postal Museum, making this the first federal building in DC to be named for an African American woman. In 2017, the United States Postal Service issued the 40th stamp in the Black Heritage series, featuring Dr. Dorothy Height, the equal rights trailblazer.

Address 2 Massachusetts Avenue NE, Washington, DC 20002, +1 (202) 633-5555, www.postalmuseum.si.edu | Getting there Metro to Union Station (Red Line); DC Circulator to Union Station, or bus 96, D6, X8 to Columbus Circle | Hours Daily 10am – 5:30pm | Tip The Mary McLeod Bethune Council House was the first headquarters of the National Council of Negro Women (1318 Vermont Avenue NW, www.nps.gov/mamc/index.htm).

21__Dumbarton House

National Society of The Colonial Dames of America

A first glimpse into Dumbarton House tells the obvious story of Martha Nourse and her husband Joseph, who lived there between 1804 and 1813. As the first Register of the US Treasury, Joseph Nourse and his family settled in the newly established capital city of Washington. Their Federal period house in Georgetown still stands as a historic museum recognizing the lifestyle of this one wealthy family, but visitors must look beyond the Nourse family to truly understand the significance of this cultural site.

Dumbarton House is a monument to historic preservation. It's an ever-changing institution that continues to redefine historiography by serving as both a national archive, as well as a cultural hub that hosts special events, like weddings, yoga classes, and markets. The house is a tangible interpretation of one of the oldest neighborhoods in the United States. Everything from the paint and brickwork to family documents and letters is studied and archived, each analysis offering more perspective about early America and connecting it with the people who continue to shape Georgetown.

These historical methods led to the discovery of a set of White Chinese export porcelain that dates back to the year 1790. The pot de crème, sweetmeat dish, and fruit basket were inherited by "Eliza" Custis Law from her grandmother, first lady Martha Washington, and used at Mount Vernon.

In 1928, the house became headquarters for the National Society of The Colonial Dames of America (NSCDA). This non-profit women's organization was established in 1891 and stores over 10,000 documents such as meeting notes, brochures, and registration records inside Dumbarton House. The NSCDA promotes the importance of historic preservation, patriotic service, and educational projects, including raising funds for the Spanish American War Monument in Arlington National Cemetery.

Address 2715 Q Street NW, Washington, DC 20007, +1 (202) 337-2288, www.dumbartonhouse.org | **Getting there** Metro to Dupont Circle (Red Line); bus D1, D2, D3, D6, G2, or DC Circulator to 28th Street NW | **Hours** See website | **Tip** Visit Montrose Park and stroll along the tree-lined Ropewalk, originally created for making rope and twine (3052 R Street NW, www.nps.gov/places/montrose-park.htm).

22 Dumbarton Oaks Park

Beatrix Jones Farrand designed gardens for Bliss

A 27-acre pastoral oasis in the heart of historic Georgetown, Dumbarton Oaks Park is not just a natural wonder, but also the living legacy of a nearly forgotten figure. The park is the masterwork of Beatrix Jones Farrand, America's first female landscape architect and the only female founding member of the American Society of Landscape Architects, and it is her only remaining wild landscape.

Farrand was born into an upper-class family in New York and grew up with an interest in garden design. Her education in landscaping was self-developed and included a European grand tour and an apprenticeship with a leading landscape architect. Farrand built herself a career spanning over 200 designs, including work on the campuses of Yale and Princeton and gardens for the White House during Woodrow Wilson's presidency.

The park was the result of a decades-long partnership between Beatrix Ferrand and Mildred Bliss. Mildred and her husband Robert purchased Dumbarton Oaks in 1921, and Mildred hired Farrand to design both a formal flower garden and a naturalistic adjoining park. This work would last over 20 years, and a bond developed between the two women. Mildred and Beatrix called themselves "gardening twins" and exchanged thousands of letters and drawings.

The upper garden is today part of Dumbarton Oaks and is a testament to Farrand's skill with formal garden settings. The adjoining park, though, is where she truly shines. Inspired by Victorian wild gardens, Farrand transformed a neglected landscape into "the illusion of country life within the city." The grounds include waterfalls, wildflower gardens, ponds, woodlands, and meadows, dotted with stone stairs and archways. Dumbarton Oaks Park was gifted to the NPS in 1940. Farrand wrote park guidelines known as the *Plant Book* for maintaining her work, and today, the park is being restored to her original vision.

Address 3100 R Street NW, Washington, DC 20007, +1 (202) 333-3547, www.dopark.org, info@dopark.org | **Getting there** Bus 30N, 30S, 31, 33 to Wisconsin Avenue & R Street NW | **Hours** Daily dusk–dawn | **Tip** Explore Beatrix Farrand's formal upper garden design and learn more about the life of Mildred Bliss at the Dumbarton Oaks Museum and Estate (1703 32nd Street NW, www.doaks.org).

23 Eleanor Roosevelt Statue

A syndicated newspaper columnist

Eleanor Roosevelt is one of the most recognized first ladies in US history, perhaps because she wrote nearly three decades' worth of memoirs that future generations continue to read. Her intriguing newspaper column *My Day* is a primary account of how she became a beloved public figure.

She wrote new stories six days a week for more than 25 years. Over 90 newspapers published her columns each day, inviting nearly four million readers into the White House. Eleanor Roosevelt's loyal readers depended on her insider political analysis and opinions about social reform. Her words offered consistent comfort to Americans throughout World War II, although she suddenly stopped writing for almost a full week in April 1945 because she had learned about the passing of her husband, President Franklin D. Roosevelt.

Eleanor returned to her column with these words: "Any man in public life is bound, in the course of years, to create certain enemies. But when he is gone, his main objectives stand out clearly and one may hope that a spirit of unity may arouse the people and their leaders to a complete understanding of his objectives and a determination to achieve those objectives themselves."

Deep inside President Roosevelt's memorial stands a grand statue of Eleanor Roosevelt with an inscription recognizing her service as a delegate to the United Nations. Created by artist Neil Estern, her statue is one of only two honoring an American woman on outdoor public land in Washington, DC. The other is Mary McLeod Bethune (see ch. 56), who was frequently mentioned in the *My Day* columns. "Mrs. Bethune told us she is now 74 years old; and I could not help hoping that, if I reached that age some years from now, I would have as much faith in human beings and in their powers of achievement."

At 76 years old, Roosevelt was awarded the Mary McLeod Bethune Human Rights Award (see ch. 56).

THE STRUCTURE
OF WORLD PEACE
CANNOT BE THE
WORK OF ONE MAN,
OR ONE PARTY,
OR ONE NATION...
IT MUST BE A PEACE
WHICH RESTS ON
THE COOPERATIVE
EFFORT OF THE
WHOLE WORLD.

ELEANOR ROOSEVELT,
FIRST UNITED STATES DELEGATE
TO THE UNITED NATIONS

Address 400 West Basin Drive SW, Washington, DC 20002, www.nps.gov/frde/index.htm, +1 (202) 426-6841 | Getting there Metro to Smithsonian (Blue, Orange, and Silver Line); DC Circulator to Franklin Delano Roosevelt Memorial | Hours Unrestricted | Tip Visit Congressional Cemetery to pay your respects at the final resting place of journalist "Cokie" Roberts, born Mary Martha Corinne Morrison Claiborne Boggs. Explore other notable women on the self-guided tour, "Women of Art and Letters" (1801 E Street SE, www.congressionalcemetery.org).

24 Ellen Wilson Place

From alley to activism, from displacement to home

Nestled near Barracks Row is Ellen Wilson Place, an unassuming residential block named for a woman with a complicated legacy. It belies a complex history of housing and displacement. Ellen Axson Wilson was the first wife of President Woodrow Wilson. Born and raised in Georgia, she was known for her refined tastes and fondness for art and music. After marrying Wilson in 1885, she supported his career while raising three daughters. Art was her refuge from increasing social demands, and she even had an art studio set up on the third floor of the White House.

As first lady, Ellen Wilson was influenced by having been raised in a slave-owning family in the deeply segregated South. She was horrified to discover that the Bureau of Engraving and Printing had integrated dining spaces and pushed her husband to segregate federal buildings. Ellen reached out to department chiefs directly and encouraged assigning separate facilities for employees based on race.

Her most public crusade was alleyway slums in DC, populated primarily by Black residents living in shanty houses and extreme poverty. She brought congressmen and socialites to encourage improvement of the living conditions in neighborhoods viewed as blighted, resulting in legislation known as "Mrs. Wilson's Bill." The racial undertones of the bill were evident, as it called for clearing out the alleyways and turning them into public parks and included few plans for housing the displaced residents. This effort included clearing out Navy Place, an alley community once located here.

In 1941, a public housing project was built on this property, named for Ellen Wilson and open to white residents only. Dozens of Black families were forced out of their homes. It remained segregated until 1953 and was eventually torn down in 1996. In 1999, a mixed-income development was opened and today is home to an array of Capitol Hill residents.

Address 6th Street & Ellen Wilson Place SE, Washington, DC 20003 | **Getting there** Metro to Eastern Market (Blue, Orange, and Silver Line); bus 90, 92 to 8th & G Streets SE | **Hours** Unrestricted | **Tip** Blagden Alley is a perfect example of how alleys are being embraced again by cities for residential space. Local architect Suzane Reatig is responsible for apartments in this buzzy alley spot (Blagden Alley NW).

25 — Enid A. Haupt Garden

A special Eden gifted by a publishing heiress

When you step into the four acres of the Enid A. Haupt Garden, nestled between the Smithsonian Castle and bustling Independence Avenue, you may not realize that you are actually enjoying a rooftop garden. Although visitors enter from street level, beneath their feet are the National Museum of African Art, the Arthur M. Sackler Gallery, and the S. Dillon Ripley Center. This garden, opened in 1987, weaves in the influences of these museums as well as the trailblazing woman for whom it is named.

Enid A. Haupt was born into a well-established publishing family that owned countless magazines and newspapers. Enid would find herself drawn to the family business, becoming the second editor of *Seventeen Magazine*, one of the first nationwide magazines to target teenage girls and encourage them to be model workers and citizens. As her fortune grew, so did her philanthropy. Her interest in horticulture led her to build and restore gardens across the country, known as Enid's Edens. Her generous contribution and guidance allowed the Smithsonian Institution to reimagine this quadrangle as an urban oasis for the public.

The centerpiece of the garden is the Parterre, a carefully manicured green space that changes with the seasons, meant to complement the stately Smithsonian Castle building. The Moongate Garden was inspired by the architecture of the Temple of Heaven in Beijing with the Fountain Garden drawing its inspiration from the Court of Lions at Alhambra, a Moorish palace in Spain. Circular pools dot the entire space, referencing the windows of the African Art building. The garden is framed by the Renwick Gates, named for James Renwick Jr., architect of the Smithsonian Castle building, and based on his design. If you peer closely at the gates, you will see a small bronze plaque honoring Enid A. Haupt and her generosity in bringing this garden to life.

Address 1050 Independence Avenue NW, Washington, DC 20560, +1 (202) 633-2220, www.gardens.si.edu/gardens/haupt-garden, gardens@si.edu | Getting there Metro to L'Enfant Plaza (Blue, Green, Orange, Silver, and Yellow Line); bus 881 to Independence Avenue NW & L'Enfant Plaza | Hours Daily dawn–dusk | Tip Stroll next door to visit the Kathrine Dulin Folger Rose Garden. Originally designed to showcase modern roses, it has evolved into a garden for roses, symbiotic plants, and insect life (990 Jefferson Drive SW, www.gardens.si.edu/gardens/folger-rose-garden).

26 The Extra Mile

Juliette "Daisy" Gordon, the Girl Scouts' founder

Along the sidewalks of downtown DC, look for a series of bronze medallions embedded at your feet. You are walking along The Extra Mile – Points of Light Volunteer Pathway. It is a mile-long tribute that honors 33 Americans who transformed the nation through service. There are 16 women honored here, including a socialite who founded the Girl Scouts of the USA.

On the eve of the Civil War, Juliette "Daisy" Gordon was born in Savannah, Georgia into a wealthy and influential family. She was an adventurous girl with particular interest in athletics, nature, animals, and the arts. As was customary for the era, her upbringing focused on molding her into a "proper" wife and mother. She married William Low, who was a family friend, in 1886 and endured almost 20 years of misery with a man who was distant, drank excessively, and had affairs. After Low's death, Juliette found herself a childless widow with a desire to serve.

In 1911, Juliette met Sir Robert Baden-Powell, founder of the Scout Movement, and they became close friends. Inspired by his work in Europe, she saw the need for a similar organization in the US. She called a cousin to say, "I've got something for the girls of Savannah and all of America and, and all the world, and we're going to start tonight!" The Girl Scouts of the USA started as a small gathering of diverse girls in 1912 and grew into the world's most prominent organization dedicated solely to girls.

Juliette worked tirelessly to build an inclusive organization with her talent for networking, fundraising, and promotion. During World War I, she pioneered a program for her scouts to grow and harvest their own food and make surgical bandages for the Red Cross (see ch. 90). Juliette led the organization until her death in 1927. She was buried in her Scout uniform and with a note stating, "You are not only the first Girl Scout, but the best Girl Scout of them all."

Address 1430 G Street NW, Washington, DC 20005, www.pointsoflight.org/the-extra-mile-points-of-light-volunteer-pathway | Getting there Metro to Metro Center (Blue, Orange, Red, and Silver Line); bus 30N, 30S, 32, 33, 36 to 15th & F Streets NW | Hours Unrestricted | Tip Look for the medallion honoring Helen Keller, disability rights activist, author, and guiding force of the American Foundation of the Blind (1450 G Street NW).

THE EXTRA MILE

Juliette Gordon Low

FOUNDED GIRL SCOUTS OF THE UNITED STATES OF AMERICA IN 1912 TO ENCOURAGE GIRLS TO DEVELOP AND STRENGTHEN THEIR LEADERSHIP SKILLS; TO PROVIDE SUPPORT, KINDNESS AND COMPASSION TO THOSE IN NEED; AND TO PREPARE TO SERVE AS RESPONSIBLE CITIZENS OF THEIR COMMUNITY AND COUNTRY. HER EFFORTS HAVE ENABLED MILLIONS OF GIRLS, FROM 5 TO 17, TO ENJOY FUN, FRIENDSHIP AND LEARNING OPPORTUNITIES IN A NURTURING ENVIRONMENT.

"The work of today is the history of tomorrow, and we are its makers."

OCTOBER 31, 1860 JANUARY 17, 1927

Points of Light Volunteer Pathway

27 Farragut Square

The teenage artist behind the masculine statues

In a square that bears his name, Admiral David Farragut's bronze statue looms over the park from atop a formidable granite base. The imposing figure echoes many military statues found in our nation's capital, but this particular work was created by a female artist who would captivate the city.

Lavinia Ellen Ream, known as Vinnie, moved to DC in 1861. As a teenager, she began working for the United States Post Office to help support her family. She was soon introduced to noted sculptor Clark Mills, who took Ream in as an apprentice. In 1864, Ream convinced President Abraham Lincoln to model for her over several months. She knew that a teenage girl sculpting the President was newsworthy and began promoting herself and her work.

After Lincoln's assassination, Congress sought an artist to create a full-size marble statue of Lincoln for the Capitol. Ream would become the youngest artist and the first woman to receive a commission as an artist for Congress, using the previous bust made from life as her entry. Her selection was controversial, given her age and inexperience – and also because she was a beautiful woman with an interest in politics.

It would take Vinnie Ream five years to complete her statue of Lincoln, as she traveled across Europe to study, and the spotlight followed her wherever she went. When the statue was unveiled in the United States Capitol Rotunda on January 25, 1871, the 23-year-old sculptor was praised for her work. That praise did not always translate to other jobs though. Her gender and youth inspired enemies to spread untrue rumors that her prized Lincoln statue had been done by Italian craftsmen.

Ream ceased most of her sculpting once she married in 1878, likely at her husband's request. She occasionally lobbied for major projects, including appealing personally to General William Sherman and Mrs. Farragut to sculpt the Farragut memorial, dedicated in 1881.

Address 912 17th Street NW, Washington, DC 20006, www.goldentriangledc.com/initiative/ farragut-park | Getting there Metro to Farragut West (Blue, Orange, Red, and Silver Line) or Farragut North (Red Line) | Hours Unrestricted | Tip You can find Vinnie Ream's statue of Abraham Lincoln in the Rotunda at the United States Capitol Building, as well as her statue of Cherokee polymath Sequoyah in National Statuary Hall. Tour tickets are required and can be reserved online (First Street NE, www.visitthecapitol.gov/plan-visit/book-tour-capitol).

28 Federal District Markers

The Garden Club of America welcomes you to DC

As the United States was celebrating the bicentennial of George Washington's birthday in 1932–1933, citizens across the country sought ways to honor "the first American." At the forefront of this effort were women's organizations and civic clubs, who worked tirelessly to raise funds and establish historical markers, plaques, and statues in towns and cities, big and small.

As you cross the border between Maryland and the District of Columbia, you can spot examples of such markers. What today look like abandoned concrete pylons are actually ceremonial entrance markers officially denoting to travelers that they have crossed the border into the Federal District. These markers were the work of the Garden Club of America, founded in 1913 by Elizabeth Price Martin.

Elizabeth Martin was a fervent supporter of historical preservation, with a particular interest in environmental conservation and horticulture. She first founded the Garden Club of Philadelphia in 1904. By 1913, 12 garden clubs in various cities signed an agreement to form the Garden Guild, later known as the Garden Club of America. Their primary mission was to record and preserve the history of American gardens, using diligent research as the foundation of their early years' work. During the George Washington Bicentennial Celebration, the group turned its attention to projects honoring Washington, including funding the DC entrance markers.

The markers are made from Aquia Creek sandstone, which was chosen by George Washington as the primary material for the city's government buildings. They bear the Maryland seal, along with a bas-relief of George Washington standing with Lady Justice. The figures are joined by a laurel wreath, a rising sun, and the Capitol building dome. In addition to the set at Chevy Chase Circle, you can find the others on Georgia Avenue, Westmoreland Circle, and Wisconsin Avenue.

Address Chevy Chase Circle NW, Washington, DC 20015, https://historicsites. dcpreservation.org/items/show/228 | **Getting there** Bus 1, 11, 401 to Western Avenue & Oliver Street NW | **Hours** Unrestricted | **Tip** The Francis Scott Key Memorial Bridge, with its great views of the Potomac, was erected by the National Society US Daughters of 1812 in memory of the man who wrote "The Star-Spangled Banner" (Francis Scott Key Bridge & M Street NW, www.nps.gov/places/000/francis-scott-key-bridge.htm).

29 Female Union Band Society

Burial ground for a band of sisters

The Female Union Band Society Cemetery has survived against all odds, proving that this Georgetown burial site is one of the most remarkable stories in American history. The resilience of this sacred cemetery to remain in existence since 1842 is a testament to the strength of the women who are interred there.

The Society began as an organized effort by mostly African American and Native American women, who banded together to offer mutual aid to one another. These free women collaborated with a man named Joseph Mason to purchase the land for $250 so that they could rest in peace, power, and union together. This cooperative benevolent society drafted their Constitution and pledged to provide each member with a grave, $20 for funeral services, and $2 per week during illness.

One astounding truth of their story is just how rare an African American cemetery was prior to the Civil War. The cemetery church served as a stop on the Underground Railroad and would supply clothing made by women who gathered in local sewing circles.

Mindful visitors should consider the delicate nature of the burial ground. The valleys mark spots where people are interred there, some buried without headstones, some stones broken or sunken into the ground, and some stolen by locals to use as coffee tables. This was not an unlikely occurrence at one point in time, according to Executive Director Lisa Fager, who also confirmed that one stone has been returned. The unmarked burial plots are a challenge historians face, as well as the fact that the cemetery pre-dates death records by 32 years.

The land also suffers from drainage problems, perhaps from nearby Rock Creek Park that was developed with land acquired from the cemetery through eminent domain. The cemetery shares property and history with Mount Zion Cemetery, established in 1808.

Address 2501 Mill Road NW, Washington, DC 20007, +1 (202) 253-0435, www.mtzion-fubs.org, info@mtzion-fubs.org | Getting there Metro to Dupont Circle (Red Line); bus D1, D2, D3, D6, G2; or DC Circulator to 28th Street NW | Hours Unrestricted | Tip The Sarah Rittenhouse Armillary Sphere is a memorial erected by the Georgetown Garden Club in honor of the woman considered to be the founder of Montrose Park (R Street & Avon Place NW, www.ncpc.gov/memorials/detail/92).

30 First Ladies Water Garden

A hidden oasis to honor women in the spotlight

"The First Lady is an unpaid public servant elected by one person – her husband."– Lady Bird Johnson

The United States Botanic Garden is the oldest continuously operating botanic garden in the country and home to over 65,000 plants. The gardens extend both inside the Conservatory and outside along the grounds. As you experience this fragrant world of plants, you may find yourself exploring the three-acre National Garden, home to the First Ladies Water Garden, the only memorial recognizing American First Ladies.

In May of 1994, six of the seven living first ladies – Hillary Clinton, Barbara Bush, Nancy Reagan, Rosalynn Carter, Betty Ford, and Lady Bird Johnson – gathered for the National Garden gala to support efforts to create a new outdoor garden on the west side of the Conservatory. The only living First Lady not in attendance was Jacqueline Kennedy Onassis, who was in poor health and would pass away a few weeks later. In 2006, First Lady Laura Bush stated in her opening ceremony remarks that the water garden "pays tribute to some of America's most extraordinary women."

The granite design of the fountain is based on the classic Colonial quilt pattern used by Martha Washington at her home of Mount Vernon. As the first woman to occupy this unique role, Martha set many of the precedents we expect from a First Lady today: supporting veterans and military families, hosting salons and events open to the public, and serving as the official hostess of the nation.

The first ladies of our nation have been tremendous women. While not always the spouse of the President of the United States, they have stepped into a role with no definition in our Constitution but the weight of the public's expectations on their shoulders. The First Ladies Water Garden provides a quiet, contemplative space to consider their work, often unnoticed and unrecognized.

Address 100 Maryland Avenue SW, Washington, DC 20001, +1 (202) 225-8333, www.usbg.gov, usbg@aoc.gov | Getting there Metro to Federal Center SW (Blue, Orange, and Silver Line); bus 30N, 30S, 32, 36 to Independence & Washington Avenues SW | Hours Daily 7:30am–5pm | Tip Nearby on the Capitol Grounds is a Chinese kousa dogwood planted by Lady Bird Johnson in 1968. Lady Bird is known for her love of horticulture and her initiative to beautify America's highways (Capitol Square NE, www.aoc.gov/explore-capitol-campus).

31 The First Woman Marine

Opha May Jacob Johnson served her country

If Washington, DC declared an official holiday honoring Opha May Jacob Johnson, it would most certainly have to be scheduled on August 13th. On that day in 1918, she became the first woman to enlist in the United States Marine Corps – a year before women were granted full federal voting rights in the United States.

At 40 years of age, Johnson was first in line with more than 300 women behind her at Headquarters Marine Corps in Washington, DC, each prepared to serve her patriotic duty during the world's Great War. Johnson was a daughter determined to follow in the footsteps of her father, a Civil War veteran, when she submitted her application for military service. Records now indicate that the document had been edited to replace all of the default "he" pronouns with more appropriate "she" pronouns. Johnson would become a clerk in the Quartermaster's Office, with increasing responsibilities that led to her promotion to sergeant within a few months. She dedicated herself to a full career in civil service, but her accomplishments went unnoticed for decades.

Johnson died in 1955 at Mount Alto Veterans Hospital, a building that originally housed an all-girls science school. She was buried in an unmarked grave in Rock Creek Cemetery on August 13, 1955, the 37th anniversary of her enlistment. Her husband, Victor Hugo Johnson, rests next to her. The two had lived together in the Mount Pleasant neighborhood. Victor worked as a music director of the Lafayette Square Opera House in Washington, DC and would introduce her at concerts as "the first female Marine."

In August of 2018, Johnson and her husband were honored with a proper headstone, in the shape of an obelisk, that clearly notes her military milestone. The effort was led by the Women Marines Association on the centennial anniversary of Sergeant Johnson's historical enlistment in the US Marine Corps.

OPHA
MAY
JACOB
JOHNSON

4 May 1879 - 11 Aug. 1955
FIRST WOMAN MARINE

Victor H. Johnson
1873 - 1950

OPHA MAY
JACOB
JOHNSON
SERGEANT
USMC
WWI

JACOB

Address 201 Allison Street NW, Washington, DC 20011, +1 (202) 726-2080,
www.rockcreekcemetery.org | Getting there Metro to Georgia Avenue-Petworth (Green
and Yellow Line); bus H8 to Rock Creek Church Road NW & Varnum Street NW |
Hours Daily 8am–7pm | Tip Explore the adjacent National Cemetery to discover the
headstone (Site O Plot 9) of WWI nurse Agnes H. von Kurowsky, the love interest of
Ernest Hemingway and inspiration for his novel *A Farewell to Arms* (21 Harewood Road
NW, www.nps.gov/nr/travel/national_cemeteries).

32_ Flora Molton Call Box

A street corner tribute for a street corner icon

If you walk the city's streets, you are likely to come across a call box. These metal structures dotting the street corners were once part of a vast alarm system used to signal for police or fire services for almost a century before going out of use and falling into disrepair. In 2019, the city undertook a project to convert eight call boxes into eight memorials to significant DC women. Local artist Charles Bergen retrofitted each box with a cast iron sculpture of a notable woman, along with paintings, symbols, sculptures, and quotes to tell her story. Noted historian Mara Cherkasky helped select the subjects, choosing women from a variety of backgrounds and eras.

Flora Molton is not a name that many Washingtonians will know, but her voice used to ring out loud and clear through the busy rush hour streets of downtown DC. A partially blind native of Louisa County, Virginia, Flora grew up surrounded by music. She learned to play the slide guitar with a knife, a technique she picked up from local musicians, and accompanied herself with a tambourine at her feet. She made her way to DC and began busking on street corners in the 1940s, earning a loyal audience of passersby.

Flora played what she called "spiritual and truth" music, using her background as a preacher to infuse her bluesy country sound with gospel praise. She would set up a plastic bucket at the corner of 11th and F Streets NW, earning enough to survive for over 20 years, until she started to be awarded with grants, prizes, and prominence – legend has it that she once held a private performance for the Rolling Stones.

Her success came late in life, with her first scheduled gig inside a coffee shop at the age of 55 and her first album recorded at 79. Flora Molton would continue to sing until six months before her death in 1990. Today she is buried at the National Harmony Memorial Park in Hyattsville, Maryland.

Address G Street NW and 13th Street NW, Washington, DC 20004, https://historicsites.dcpreservation.org/items/show/1034 | Getting there Metro to Metro Center (Blue, Orange, Red, and Silver Line); bus D6 to 13th & G Streets NW | Hours Unrestricted | Tip If you walk G Street to 14th Street, you'll spot another call box, this one honoring Mary Church Terrell, an educator in DC, founder of several civil rights organizations, suffragist, activist, and more (14th and G Streets NW, https://historicsites.dcpreservation.org/tours/show/14).

33 Folger Shakespeare Library

Emily Folger's quest to preserve literary history

On Capitol Hill, inside a stately structure, sits the world's largest collection of the printed works of William Shakespeare. This immense public research library came to life thanks to the lifelong dedication of Emily Jordan Folger and her husband Henry Clay Folger.

Emily, born in 1858 in Ohio, was well-educated for the era, attending Vassar to study English composition and astronomy. She was a teacher before she and Henry married in 1885. They shared a love of literature, particularly Shakespeare and Early Modern texts.

Their vast collection began with Emily poring over booksellers' catalogs, marking items of interest, and seeking out rare folios. Once she purchased an item, she would create a catalog card for each acquisition and cross-reference the cards to avoid duplicate purchases. Emily was actively engaged in researching for their collection, corresponding with Shakespeare scholars, and joining various societies studying his work. She earned her M.A. from Vassar in 1896 with a thesis on the contemporary scholarship of the playwright.

It would take from 1918 to 1930 for the Folgers to buy the land and lay the cornerstone of their collection's public home. The stock market crash reduced the value of Henry's estate, and Emily donated millions of dollars of her own to fund the completion of the building. She became the third woman to be awarded an honorary doctorate from Amherst College for her efforts.

In 1932, the building opened to the public and Emily remained active with the library until her death in 1936. The bulk of her estate was left to support the library and today both she and Henry are interred in the Old Reading Room. She once wrote that "the poet is one of our best sources, one of the wells from which we Americans draw our national thought, our faith, and our hope."

Address 201 E Capitol Street SE, Washington, DC 20003, +1 (202) 544-4600, www.folger.edu, info@folger.edu | Getting there Metro to Union Station (Red Line) or Capitol South (Blue, Orange, and Silver Line) | Hours Mon–Sat 10am–5pm, Sun noon–5pm | Tip Satisfy your sweet tooth at nearby upscale bakery Sweet Lobby, founded by Dr. Winnette Ambrose. Ambrose is an engineer and self-taught pastry chef, who specializes in French macarons and award-winning cupcakes in her Barracks Row shop (404 8th Street SE, www.sweetlobby.com).

34 Ford's Theatre

Frankie Childers Hewitt preserved Lincoln's legacy

During a decade when families were tuning in to watch *The Carol Burnett Show* and *Bewitched*, a woman named Frankie Hewitt leveraged the power of modern television to preserve a historic venue. She founded the Ford's Theatre Society and hosted an inaugural gala nationally broadcast on January 30, 1968. Americans watched First Lady of Theater Helen Hayes take the stage for the very first performance at Ford's Theatre since President Lincoln's assassination nearly a century earlier.

Hours earlier, North Vietnam launched the Tet Offensive against South Vietnam and the US, but the show would go on, just as it did during the Civil War when President Lincoln attended Ford's Theatre at least 12 times. He said, "Some think I do wrong to go to the opera and the theater: but it rests me... A hearty laugh relieves me; and I seem better able after it to bear my cross."

Ownership of the Ford's Theatre building was transferred to the federal government and the National Park Service after Lincoln's death, but it would remain mostly a gutted storage warehouse until the 1960s. Hewitt was adamant that the venue become a living memorial to Lincoln's life. As a speech writer for John F. Kennedy, she felt inclined after his assassination to push forward with historic preservation efforts at the theater and worked in parallel to a group from Actors' Equity to renovate the venue in a way that would support live performances. Her annual galas would be a major fundraising source for a revival of Ford's Theatre.

Conspiracy enthusiasts must not miss the Mary Surratt statue (see ch. 93) in the museum or the plaque at the rear of the theater that recognizes Hewitt, who once said, "It's the perfect place to introduce young people to theater. At Ford's you get a history lesson and an arts experience." President Bush awarded her the National Humanities Medal one day before she passed.

Address 511 10th Street NW, Washington, DC 20004, +1 (202) 347-4833, www.fords.org, visit@fords.org | Getting there Metro to Metro Center (Blue, Orange, Silver, and Red Line); bus 64 to 11th & E Streets NW | Hours See website for hours and schedule | Tip Helen Hayes helped to desegregate the National Theatre, the city's oldest continuously operating theater. Visit the Helen Hayes Gallery there (1321 Pennsylvania Avenue NW, www.thenationaldc.com).

FRANKIE HEWITT
FOUNDER
FORD'S THEATRE SOCIETY
1968

The force behind the rebirth of Ford's Theatre as a thriving cultural institution.

35__ The Four Founders

Founding the Daughters of the American Revolution

Near the White House stands the headquarters of the Daughters of the American Revolution (DAR). Outside is an evocative memorial sculpted by Gertrude Vanderbilt Whitney, noted artist and DAR member. Dedicated in 1929, the memorial features a woman with outstretched arms, flanked by four medals honoring the women who made the civic society possible, turning rejection into a powerful women's organization: Mary Desha, Mary Lockwood, Ellen Walworth, and Eugenia Washington.

In 1890, the Sons of the American Revolution voted to exclude women from membership entirely. The ensuing controversy caught the eye of Mary Lockwood, who wrote a fiery editorial for the *Washington Post* asking, "Were there no mothers of the Revolution?" A call went out to form a women's lineage-based society, and four women took the helm. These women were not ladies of leisure but rather the activists and advocates of their era.

Mary Desha was an educator and advocate for Native Alaskans. She would later work for the Office of Indian Affairs, and she was the assistant director of the DAR Hospital Corps during the Spanish-American War. Mary Lockwood was a prolific author, activist for women's rights, president of the Women's Press Club, and a manager-at-large at the World's Columbian Exposition in 1893. Ellen Walworth was a suffragist lawyer, scholar of American history, and an advocate for the preservation of Mount Vernon. Eugenia Washington survived being caught in the middle of the battle of Fredericksburg and became a civil servant and historian.

These women held the first organizing meeting on October 11, 1890, where the first slate of officers was elected, including First Lady Caroline Harrison as President General. Harrison was interested in White House history and restoration, and she helped establish DAR's dedication to historic preservation, which continues today.

Address 1756 C Street NW, Washington, DC 20006, +1 (202) 628-1776, www.dar.org/ archives/four-founders | **Getting there** Metro to Farragut West (Blue, Orange, Red, and Silver Line); bus 7Y, 80 to 18th & D Streets NW | **Hours** Unrestricted | **Tip** A short walk away, you'll spot a callbox honoring Alice Paul, DAR member and founder of the National Woman's Party. Alice was a lifelong feminist advocate for women's rights and suffrage (14th and E Streets NW, https://historicsites.dcpreservation.org/tours/show/14).

36 FREED Ladies

African American Civil War Museum comes to life

Education can become more dynamic when it expands beyond the classroom. And one of the most engaging mediums for public history is re-enactment, as showcased by the FREED Ladies, a group of local women who portray their historical ancestors.

The "Female RE-Enactors of Distinction" (FREED) is an auxiliary group of the African American Civil War Museum. They met during planning meetings for the museum's Founder's Day celebration in 2005 and formed the organization to promote the accomplishments of African American Civil War soldiers and the women who supported their fight for freedom. The FREED Ladies visit schools and libraries, and they have even been spotted marching down Constitution Avenue during the annual Memorial Day parade.

Their presence catches the attention of curious observers, who notice these ladies dressed in period attire from the mid-nineteenth century Civil War era. These women are storytellers, interpreters, and re-enactors, who perform dramatic readings but also offer casual interactions with interested listeners. The hostesses are mostly women of color, but the organization's mission statement notes they are an integrated group who "welcome the portrayal of ladies from other races of the era who were abolitionists as well." Their roles are emphasized by "Distinction" to combat the myth of the general public that their "ancestors only worked in the fields in rag and wished for a brighter day."

They travel in groups, sometimes as large as 17, and all come from diverse backgrounds; a French teacher, a staffer at the State Department, and a former nurse in the United States Coast Guard, to name a few. They honor women overlooked and forgotten, such as entrepreneur Elleanor Eldridge, feminist activist Hallie Quinn Brown, and Dr. Rebecca Davis Lee Crumpler, the first African American woman physician in the United States.

Address 1925 Vermont Avenue NW, Washington, DC 20001, +1 (202) 667-2667, www.afroamcivilwar.org | Getting there Metro to U Street (Green and Yellow Line); bus 64 to Vermont Avenue & U Street NW | Hours See website | Tip Elizabeth Keckley was a dressmaker and confidant to First Lady Mary Todd Lincoln. Look for the sewing needle on her public art call box installation (15th & K Streets NW, https://historicsites. dcpreservation.org/items/show/1039).

37 The Furies Collective

The L words: Lesbians, Literature, and Liberation

In the summer of 1971, a group of lesbians embarked on a radical mission. They established the Furies Collective, living, working, and publishing together out of three houses, including a brick townhouse on Capitol Hill, from 1971 to 1973. Though short-lived, the group had a tremendous influence on the social movements of the day.

Fresh off the Stonewall riots of 1969, there was renewed interest in finding safe spaces for lesbians and gays to live, work, and create. The Furies – named for the Greek female spirits of Justice and Vengeance – formed after publishing a lesbian edition of *motive*, a youth magazine and chose their Southeast location because it was gay-friendly and accessible to the group's needs.

They established a lesbian, feminist, separatist collective with 12 core members and published a tabloid-sized newspaper titled *The Furies*, which specifically addressed questions about women's identities and their relationships with other women, men, and society. They advocated for a separatist philosophy, encouraging lesbian feminists to make their way independent of the existing women's movement and gay rights movements, both of which could be exclusionary of lesbians.

The Furies were also community oriented. They lived and worked in a communal state, sharing resources, supplies, and talents. They taught classes on self-defense, basic home repair, and language instruction in English and Spanish to women of all backgrounds to build self-reliance among their sex.

While the group itself burned fast and bright, their influence was immeasurable. The ideas and writings of the Furies Collective had an impact on the gay rights and women's movements of the 1970s and beyond. Their former home, now privately owned, is the first lesbian-related historic landmark named in DC, and it was the first lesbian-specific site on the National Register of Historic Places.

Address 219 11th Street SE, Washington, DC 20003, www.nps.gov/places/furies-collective.htm | **Getting there** Metro to Eastern Market (Blue, Orange, and Silver Line); bus 90, 92 to 8th Street & Independence Avenue SE | **Hours** Viewable from the outside only | **Tip** When historic sports bar Phase One closed in 2016, queer women had limited options for their own space until A League of Her Own opened in 2018. The low-key sports bar fosters a fun, inclusive environment with foosball, pool, and video games (2319 18th Street NW, www.pitchersbardc.com).

THE FURIES HOUSE
A RADICAL LESBIAN
FEMINIST COLLECTIVE
CIRCA 1972
HAS BEEN PLACED ON THE
NATIONAL REGISTER
OF HISTORIC PLACES
BY THE UNITED STATES
DEPARTMENT OF THE INTERIOR

38 GALA Hispanic Theatre

Rebecca Read tells the story of Latino culture

Since 1976, GALA Hispanic Theatre (Grupo de Artistas Latino-Americanos) has worked to promote Latino arts and cultures by developing and producing works that explore the breadth of Latino experiences. Originally based in an Adams Morgan townhouse, the Theatre eventually found a permanent home in historic Tivoli Square. The Tivoli Theatre, built in 1924 and shut down in 1976 due to civil unrest, became home to GALA in 2005, merging cultures and history into one dynamic, layered space.

Hugo Medrano came to Washington from Argentina and began working with Teatro Doble, a bilingual children's theater. There, he met Rebecca Read, a dancer, and the two immediately recognized the need for Spanish-speaking theater for a Latino audience, especially in a city where almost 20% of the population identifies as Hispanic. They would spearhead the creation of GALA together – and get married along the way. GALA has produced nearly 300 bilingual productions, including commissioned works by emerging Latino performing artists, and won countless local, regional, and national awards. The shows are presented in Spanish with English captioning in large text, making their performances inclusive for a wide range of audience members.

Inclusivity is at the heart of Rebecca Read Medrano's vision. Rebecca has served as GALA's executive director since its founding. She has developed programming geared towards DC's youth, who are welcome at Paso Nuevo and GALita Children's Theatre. She established international exchanges with theaters in Spain, Mexico, Venezuela, and Argentina. Her vision is collaborative, and she is known for championing the work of other performing arts groups. As Rebecca says, "We need our niche. We need the culturally specific theaters, we need the Afro-centric theatre, we need all the groups large and small to band together and help one another and create partnerships."

Address 3333 14th Street NW, Washington, DC 20010, +1 (202) 234-7174, www.galatheatre.org, info@galatheatre.org | Getting there Metro to Columbia Heights (Green and Yellow Line); bus 52, 54, 59 to 14th & Monroe Streets NW | Hours See website for schedule | Tip Explore the spirit of Cuba at the Colada Shop, founded by Daniella Senior. Enjoy coffee, sweets, sandwiches, and more in a casual café setting with a rooftop bar (1405 T Street NW, www.coladashop.com).

39 _ Gallaudet Memorial

Alice Cogswell, inspiration to Thomas Gallaudet

Thomas Hopkins Gallaudet was meant to be a minister. When he graduated from Andover Theological Seminar in 1814, he planned to become a preacher. His entire life changed when he met Alice Cogswell, the nine-year-old daughter of a neighbor. Alice had contracted spotted fever when she was two years old and lost her ability to hear. She was bright and inquisitive, but while her sisters would play with Gallaudet's children, Alice would often sit alone in the garden. Gallaudet started trying to communicate with her, using sticks to draw images in the dirt or pantomiming.

Gallaudet was inspired by Alice to travel to Europe to study methods for educating deaf students. He was most impressed with the results he saw from manual communication in Paris and learned sign language himself. When Gallaudet returned to America with Deaf French teacher Laurent Clerc, they embarked on a fundraising tour to found a school for hearing-impaired students. It would become known as the American School for the Deaf (originally the Connecticut Asylum for the Education and Instruction for Deaf and Dumb Persons). Alice Cogswell was one of the first students. It was at this school where the basis of American Sign Language was formed. Alice graduated in 1824 and became an ambassador for the school. Sadly, she died of pneumonia at just 25 in 1830.

In 1857, Gallaudet's son would become the first president of Gallaudet College, renamed as such in 1894 from the National Deaf Mute College to honor Thomas Gallaudet for his life's work. On the south end of campus, there is a statue sculpted by Daniel Chester French, who created the Lincoln Memorial. The work features Gallaudet with young Alice and acknowledges the special bond between teacher and student that revolutionized deaf education around the world. The statue was a gift to the college from the National Association of the Deaf in 1889.

Address 800 Florida Avenue NE, Washington, DC 20002, +1 (202) 651-5000, www.gallaudet.edu, welcome.center@gallaudet.edu | Getting there Metro to NoMa-Gallaudet (Red Line); bus 90, 92 to Florida Avenue & 8th Street NE | Hours Contact for visiting information | Tip The Hanson Plaza and Dining Hall at Gallaudet is named for Agatha Tiegel Hanson. She was the first woman to graduate from Gallaudet with a four-year degree and the first female class valedictorian (800 Florida Avenue NE, www.gallaudet.edu).

40 — Grave of Alice Birney
Founder of the PTA rests at Oak Hill Cemetery

Founded in 1848 by banker William Corcoran, Oak Hill Cemetery was established as a rural burial ground on the outskirts of Georgetown. The first person laid to rest in the tranquil setting was Eleanor Ann Washington, the great grandniece of President George Washington, and her lineage set a tone for those to follow. It became the final resting place for politicians, diplomats, socialites, and philanthropists. Ornate Victorian-style monuments and memorials dot the landscape, with a Gothic Revival-style chapel designed by James Renwick near the entrance.

Among the markers visitors will see that bear the names of cabinet secretaries, journalists, and spies, is one that is inscribed *Alice McLellan Birney*. Although her name may not be particularly familiar to you, the organization she founded likely is – the PTA.

Alice was born in Georgia in 1858 with a passion for education. She attended Mount Holyoke College and worked as a schoolteacher and social worker. After her first husband died, she married Theodore Birney in 1892, who encouraged her interest in child development. She became friendly with wealthy widow Phoebe Hearst, the mother of publisher William Randolph Hearst. Alice discovered that Phoebe shared her interest in founding an organization that would bring an enlightened approach to education. She provided the educational experience and acumen; Hearst, the financial assistance.

In 1897, the National Congress of Mothers held its first meeting in DC, with over 2,000 attendees. The group, later known as the National Congress of Mothers and Parent-Teacher Associations (PTA), grew immensely at the grassroots level in its first five years with Alice McLellan Birney serving as president. Birney stepped back from leading the organization due to declining health, and she spent the last few years of her life writing books, articles, and pamphlets on parenting and education.

Address 3001 R Street NW, Washington, DC 20007, +1 (202) 337-2835,
www.oakhillcemeterydc.org, info@oakhillcemeterydc.org | **Getting there** Bus D2, D6
to Q & 30th Streets NW | **Hours** Mon–Fri 9am–4:30pm, Sat 11am–4pm, Sun 1–4pm |
Tip Also buried at Oak Hill is Georgetown resident E.D.E.N. (Emma Dorothy Eliza Devitt)
Southworth, who published more than 60 novels and was one of the most popular novelists
of her era (Lot 534).

41 Hidden Figures Way
Black women's contributions to space exploration

Author Margot Lee Shetterly elevated women in the fields of math and science when she wrote her book *Hidden Figures* and uncovered the forgotten history of Black women who contributed to American space exploration. These women worked in segregated offices located in the West Area of the Langley Memorial Aeronautical Laboratory in Hampton, Virginia, the same town where Shetterly spent her childhood. Her father served as a climate expert for the National Aeronautics and Space Administration (NASA).

Shetterly learned from an early age that the face of science was diverse in race and gender. Her *New York Times* best-selling book was adapted into a hit movie and became a nation-wide symbol of progress. In June 2019, NASA marked this monumental story by renaming the street in front of their headquarters "Hidden Figures Way."

While many women identify as "hidden figures" during this era, there are three ladies most often cited as such. Another notable woman from Hampton was Mary Jackson who is recognized as the first African American engineer at NASA and became the namesake of the Washington, DC headquarters building in June 2020. Portrayed in the movie alongside Jackson was Dorothy Vaughan. This hidden figure left her teaching job in 1943 to accept a position at the laboratory. Vaughan was promoted in 1949 to become the first Black supervisor at NACA, the agency that predated the formation of NASA, which became integrated in 1958.

The final of the three is mathematician Katherine Johnson, recipient of the Presidential Medal of Freedom for calculating the trajectories of the first moon landing. Portraying her character in the movie was actress Taraji P. Henson, who was born in Washington, DC and paid her way through Howard University by working days at the Pentagon and nights as a performer on the *Spirit of Washington* dinner-cruise ship on the Potomac River.

Address 4th & E Streets SW, Washington, DC 20546, +1 (202) 358-0001, www.nasa.gov | Getting there Metro to Federal Center SW (Blue, Orange, and Silver Line); bus P6 to 4th & E Streets SE | Hours Unrestricted | Tip Go for a stroll along the picturesque waterfront nearby and get a sweet treat at Southwest Soda Pop Shop, a Black-owned business and family-operated ice cream shop managed by four daughters and their father (1142 Maine Avenue SW, www.swsodapopshop.com).

42 Hillwood Estate

Marjorie Merriweather Post's lost Smithsonian

The infamous Mar-a-Lago in Palm Beach, Florida was built to be the winter estate of Marjorie Merriweather Post, owner of Post Cereal Company. She was influential in establishing the frozen foods market, an innovation that would ultimately benefit women in the domestic sphere. She acquired much wealth and invested into philanthropic ventures, art collections, and real estate. She owned properties all across the United States and traveled the world often but established a permanent home in Washington, DC. Her legacy remains tucked away in Rock Creek Park at Hillwood Estate, Museum & Gardens, where she died in 1973.

Even before she passed away, Post was curating her home to become a museum available to the public and even offered docent-led tours throughout the 1960s. She spent a lifetime collecting Russian imperial art, French decorative art, and valuable objects like jewels and gold boxes. A quote featured near the entrance of the visitor center reads, "I came to the realization that the collection should belong to the country."

In her Last Will and Testament, Post willed her estate to the Smithsonian Institution. The offer was rejected after the Smithsonian determined that her $10-million endowment would not be enough to maintain operations. The estate was reclaimed by the Marjorie Merriweather Post Foundation and her daughters. What happened next is typical in historic preservation: these women saved this site. Her granddaughter Ellen Charles served as Chair of the Board for 25 years and is credited with shaping Hillwood Estate into a sustainable professional museum. Charles said, "My goal was to fulfill my grandmother's wishes. I had a road to go down."

Marjorie Merriweather Post left her mark on the world in no uncertain terms. She was a suffragist, divorced four times, didn't drink alcohol, and threw the best parties in town.

Address 4155 Linnean Avenue, NW Washington, DC 20008, +1 (202) 686-5807, www.hillwoodmuseum.org | Getting there Bus L1 or L2 to Connecticut Avenue and Tilden Street NW | Hours Tue–Sun 10am–5pm | Tip Washington International School is situated among Tregaron Conservancy, an oasis in the woods that was once the home of Marjorie Merriweather Post and her ex-husband (3100 Macomb Street NW, www.tregaron.org).

43 Hotel Zena

A mindfully curated feminine space

As the world was shutting down, Hotel Zena was opening up. The city's first women's empowerment hotel defied all odds when they opened their doors in 2020 during one of the hospitality industry's most devastating years. The timing is indicative of the hotel's overall message of feminine strength, hope, and perseverance. On the centennial anniversary of the 19th Amendment, Hotel Zena's presence just blocks from the White House serves as an ode to feminism and a symbolic reminder that women's history and activism are rooted in Washington, DC.

Hotel Zena is more than a hotel – it is a bold statement by curator and designer Andrea Sheehan of Dawson Design Associates. Entering the lobby feels like the first stop on a museum tour. The front desk is a glass display case full of colorful high-heel shoes, welcoming visitors to the start of what will be an interactive and visual journey of stories, art, and empowerment. The curvy interior design invites the exploration of ground floor highlights, including a particularly striking portrait of Ruth Bader Ginsburg that's almost entirely made of tampons. The Serpent installation winds around the ceiling and is a modern depiction of the Benjamin Franklin's 1754 revolutionary era cartoon, "Join, or Die." A display of protest buttons is just next to The Wall of Honor, which recognizes advocates like Greta Thunberg, Malala Yousafzai, and Hillary Clinton. The height of this experience is looking up to discover the symbolic shattered glass ceiling just next to the elevators as you head up to Hedy's Rooftop for a beautiful view.

A mural on the building's exterior is so beautiful and breathtaking that it dominates the skyline. Guardians of the Four Directions by artist MISS CHELOVE is an intriguing outdoor representation of what's inside this hub of feminine culture that celebrates women's accomplishments.

Address 1155 14th Street NW, Washington, DC 20005, +1 (202) 737-1200, www.viceroyhotelsandresorts.com/zena, zena.info@viceroyhotelsandresorts.com | Getting there Metro to McPherson Square (Blue, Orange, and Silver Line); bus 54 to 14th & L Streets NW; DC Circulator to 14th & Eye Streets NW | Hours See website for bar & lounge hours | Tip View Chanel Compton's portrait of Shirley Chisholm in Hotel Zena, and then visit her portrait by Kadir Nelson in the Capitol Building. Contact your House Representative for a tour (First Street NE, history.house.gov).

44 _ The Howard Theatre

Ladies sing the blues

When The Howard Theatre opened in 1910, it seated 1,200 patrons and was the largest theatre for African American artists in the world. In the heart of segregated DC, the opulent venue served as a showcase for these artists. Billie Holiday, Ella Fitzgerald, Moms Mabley, and Dinah Washington are just some of the notable women who performed on its stage.

In the early years, the Amateur Contest was a very popular event that showcased local talent. Ella Fitzgerald spent the early days of her rise to stardom entering such contests, including several at The Howard. Actress and singer Pearl Bailey danced in The Howard Theatre chorus line while she took vocal classes at the beginning of her career. The Supremes made one of their first appearances outside of Detroit in a Motortown Revue at The Howard in 1962.

The first integrated all-women band in the United States, the International Sweethearts of Rhythm used The Howard Theatre as one of their home theatres, and they were often top billed at the midnight shows. The group started in Mississippi, at the Piney Woods Country Life School, where many of the students were orphans. The jazz act's members ranged in age from 14 to 19 years old and dubbed themselves "international" due to the racial diversity of the group. When the band left school, they settled in Arlington, Virginia and made The Howard their base of operations. One show at the theatre in 1941 set a box office record of 35,000 patrons in a single week.

Be sure to glance down at the stretch of sidewalk between the Shaw-Howard Metro station and the theatre on T Street NW. You will find The Howard Theatre's Walk of Fame, dedicated in 2019. Hand-sculpted medallions feature prominent Black performers from Howard Theatre's history, including opera singer Abbie Mitchell, the "Queen of R&B" Ruth Brown, and famed guitarist Sister Rosette Tharpe.

Address 620 T Street NW, Washington, DC 20001, +1 (202) 803-2899, www.thehowardtheatre.com | Getting there Metro to Shaw-Howard University (Green and Yellow Line); bus 70, 79 to 7th & T Streets NW | Hours See website for schedule | Tip Leah Cheston and her husband Thor run Right Proper Brewing Company next door. The neighborhood brewpub and kitchen pairs yeast-focused beers with a bit of whimsy and excellent eats (624 T Street NW, www.rightproperbrewing.com).

45 __ Human Rights Porch

Social justice at Washington National Cathedral

Founded as a great church with national purpose, the Washington National Cathedral is the sixth largest gothic-style cathedral in the world. It is committed to both religious worship and social justice, and its Human Rights Porch features three stone carvings of women who have served the country as spiritual and cultural leaders.

Born Anna Eleanor Roosevelt, she was first lady to the President and first delegate to the United Nations. She served as committee chairperson in drafting the Universal Declaration of Human Rights. Her stone carving was dedicated on the document's 50th anniversary in 1998. Much like the cathedral's purpose and Eleanor Roosevelt's vision, the Declaration clearly states the desire for "faith in fundamental human rights."

The First Lady met with the mother of the civil rights movement, Rosa Louise McCauley Parks, the year after she was arrested for refusing to give up her seat on a segregated bus in Montgomery, Alabama (see ch. 82). Roosevelt wrote in her *My Day* column (see ch. 23) about the quiet and gentle nature of Rosa Parks while admiring her strong stance against injustice.

The stone carving of Parks serves as a testament to progress and perseverance – that a seamstress from Alabama can blaze a path all the way to the United States Capitol Building, where she became the first woman in history to lay in honor.

Rosa Parks is the companion carving to Mother Teresa of Calcutta, each looking at the other from opposite sides of the archway. Washington National Cathedral dedicated both of these memorials in 2012. Just four years later, Pope Francis officially canonized Mother Teresa as a Roman Catholic saint, a woman who was awarded the Nobel Peace prize for her humanitarian work around the world. In 1997, the US Mint issued a bronze coin replica of her Congressional Gold Medal that reads, *Service to the poorest of the poor.*

Address 3101 Wisconsin Avenue NW, Washington, DC 20016, +1 (202) 537-6200, www.cathedral.org, info@cathedral.org | Getting there Metro to Cleveland Park (Red Line), then take bus 96 to Woodley Road & Wisconsin Avenue NW, or walk 20 minutes | Hours See website for hours and services | Tip Enjoy brunch at Open City, the coffeehouse and café housed in the Old Baptistry building on the Cathedral's grounds. The menu offers a broad range of savory meals, sweet pastries, coffees and teas often sourced from local businesses (3101 Wisconsin Avenue NW, www.cathedral.org/visit-us-2/cathedral-cafe).

46 International Spy Museum

Virginia Hall, an unlikely spy with only one leg

Inside the recently relocated International Spy Museum, you will find exhibits highlighting the work of famous women like Mata Hari, Hedy Lamar, and Julia Child (see ch. 49), who have their spy stories shared alongside eye-catching artifacts like a lipstick pistol. If you look closely though, you may realize that an unassuming object tells a fascinating story.

Keep your eyes peeled for the Type III MKII Radio that Virginia Hall used during World War II. She used the suitcase radio, with headphones and morse code pads, when she parachuted into France to send coded intelligence messages to the Office of Strategic Services (OSS). This was no easy task. To generate electricity to operate the radio, she had to pedal a bike frame to charge the radio's battery. What might sound impossible was just another day at work for Hall. Born in Baltimore to a wealthy family, Hall dreamt of being a diplomat, a field mostly closed to women at the time. She was also stymied by a hunting accident that ended with her left leg amputated below the knee and replaced with a wooden leg.

Hall volunteered to drive ambulances in France in 1940, until she joined the British Special Operations Executive (SOE). She was a secret agent in Vichy, France, using the art of makeup and disguise to change her appearance frequently. She remained undercover and uncaptured for two years, a limping lady evading capture. Wanted posters with her face were posted in Lyon, calling her "The Enemy's Most Dangerous Spy." When the SOE feared she had been compromised, she worked for the OSS in 1944 and 1945, supporting the French Resistance and evaluating sites for the D-Day invasion.

Hall was ultimately awarded the Distinguished Service Cross in 1945 in recognition of her efforts and making her the most highly decorated female civilian of the war. In an attempt to remain undercover, she refused a public ceremony.

Address 700 L'Enfant Plaza SW, Washington, DC 20024, +1 (202) 393-7798, www.spymuseum.org, info@spymuseum.org | Getting there Metro to L'Enfant Plaza (Blue, Green, Orange, Silver, and Yellow Line); bus 697 to D & 9th Streets SW | Hours See website | Tip The historic Mayflower Hotel has been privy to clandestine meetings involving Nazi saboteurs, Soviet agents, and American spies. Check out the art gallery on the second floor to see first ladies, politicos, and more (1127 Connecticut Avenue NW, www.themayflowerhotel.com).

47 Jeanne d'Arc

To the women of America from the women of France

A fierce medieval warrior, suited up in body armor with a sword by her side, she was just a teenager when she led an army of French soldiers into battle during the Hundred Years War in the 1420s. Her actions were guided by divine voices in her head that directed her on a military mission to protect her country. Some could say she was the original Arya Stark, but history has it that Jeanne d'Arc, or Joan of Arc, won the war without ever having killed a single soul.

Her leadership style was feminine in nature, and she became known as the "Maid of Orleans." She thought critically about effective strategies, developed solutions, and executed decisions in a diplomatic fashion. Her presence was an inspiration to the men who followed her, but her gender-nonconforming behavior was a threat to cowardly men who opposed her. The traditional story about Joan of Arc has her captured, accused of witchery, convicted for heresy, and burned to death at the stake.

She would become an everlasting symbol in the feminism movement. Suffragists in the early twentieth century would ride atop horses and wear medieval costumes in parades. The feminine pageantry was intended to balance their militant demand for voting rights. Joan of Arc has remained a transcendent icon for centuries after her execution. In 1920, she was ultimately canonized as a saint by the Catholic Church.

Her statue in Meridian Hill Park was a gift "To the Women of America" from "The Women of France." At the dedication in 1922, President General Mrs. George Minor from the Daughters of the American Revolution (see ch. 35) accepted the statue from Madame Carlo Polifemo, who said, "Nothing more sacred could be dedicated to the women of America, nothing more beautiful offered to the beautiful city of Washington than this pious work of art. Jeanne d'Arc is a living prayer, a perfect disciple of all virtues, a divine symbol for all."

Address 16th & W Streets NW, Washington, DC 20009, www.nps.gov/places/meridian-hill-park.htm | Getting there Metro to U Street (Green and Yellow Line); bus S9 to 16th & Euclid Streets NW | Hours Unrestricted | Tip Bordering the park, the Josephine Butler Parks Center is a living tribute to the champion for DC statehood and advocate for preserving neighborhood parks (2437 15th Street NW, www.washingtonparks.net/josephine-butler-parks-center).

48 Juanita Thornton Library

Her community needed books, not burgers

A plan to build a public library to serve the Shepherd Park neighborhood first arose in 1984. The closest library was almost two miles away, and residents of the northernmost point of Northwest DC wanted a library of their own. But a library was not a priority for developers, who took advantage of swiftly changing zoning laws to demolish an apartment building, with the intention of constructing a Wendy's fast-food restaurant.

Retired local schoolteacher and community activist Juanita E. Thornton leapt into action. She shared the opinion of many residents: the neighborhood needed access to educational materials and resources, not another fast-food franchise. Thornton began to organize the community and garnered strong neighborhood support behind building a library on the site of the demolished apartments with the rallying cry, "Books, not Burgers!"

Thornton took her grassroots campaign to City Council, enlisting the support of DC Councilwoman Charlene Drew Jarvis. This was not Thornton's first experience with activism. She had been an advocate for the rights of senior citizens, lobbying for adult literacy programs for seniors and priority seating on city buses. Despite the fact that Thornton was now legally blind and no longer able to read, she became the face and voice of the library fight.

In July 1985, thanks to Thornton's persistence and dedication, the library plan was approved, though it would take five years to bring the project to life. The library was dedicated in 1990 with a collection of more than 20,000 books, tapes, records, CDs, and magazines for local residents to enjoy. Sadly, Juanita Thornton passed away just two months after the library opened. In 1992, in response to an outpouring from the community, the branch was renamed in her honor. Today, a portrait of Juanita E. Thornton is visible to everyone who enters the library that bears her name.

Address 7420 Georgia Avenue NW, Washington, DC 20012, +1 (202) 541-6100, www.dclibrary.org/thornton, shepherdparklibrary@dc.gov | Getting there Bus 70 to Georgia Avenue NW & Geranium Street NW | Hours See website | Tip One other DC public library branch is named for a woman, Dorothy Height, a civil and women's rights activist with a long history of advocacy in the city. Her funeral was held at Washington National Cathedral, where President Barack Obama delivered the eulogy (3935 Benning Road NE, www.dclibrary.org/benning).

49 Julia Child House
The celebrity chef's butter-yellow home

A home the color of butter is the perfect fit for the woman who brought French cooking to the American dining room table and changed the way we eat forever. This quaint building on Olive Street was once home to Julia Child in the 1940s and 1950s, before she became a household name.

Julia Williams wanted to serve her country during World War II, but at 6'2", she was considered too tall for military service. Instead, she volunteered for the forerunner to today's CIA, working directly for General William J. Donovan, head of the Office of Strategic Services (see ch. 46), as one of only 4,500 women in the agency. She moved to the OSS Emergency Sea Rescue Equipment Section, where she helped to develop shark repellant. She met Paul Child during this time and fell in love. In 1948, the couple bought this Georgetown home – though they didn't live here long.

Paul's career would take them to France, where Julia discovered her love of French cuisine. She graduated from the famed Cordon Bleu and began her work adapting classic French recipes and techniques to methods that American home cooks could follow. She and Paul returned to their yellow abode in 1956, and Julia's first task was to renovate the kitchen in order to have a more appropriate space to test recipes for what would become *Mastering the Art of French Cooking*. She would revise the manuscript in this house, while making money teaching French cooking classes to local women.

By the time her famous cookbook was published in 1961, the Childs had sold their DC house and relocated to Cambridge, Massachusetts. Julia Child would go on to become one of the most famous faces in food, publishing numerous books, hosting television shows, and forever changing the American palate. There is one small nod to Julia Child's time in this house – the door knocker is a metal kitchen trivet, just like the original one used by Julia.

Address 2706 Olive Street NW, Washington, DC 20007 | Getting there Bus 30N, 30S, 31, 33, 38B to Pennsylvania Avenue NW & 28th Street NW; DC Circulator to M & 28th Streets NW | Hours Viewable from the outside only | Tip A visit to Julia Child's kitchen at the National Museum of American History is a must for any food fanatic. Her Cambridge kitchen was transported to the museum in 2001, fully stocked with items and gadgets she used daily (1300 Constitution Avenue NW, www.americanhistory.si.edu).

50 Justice O'Connor Portrait

Paving the way for women on the Supreme Court

The Supreme Court of the United States was established when the Judiciary Act of 1789 was signed into law. For 191 consecutive years, the highest court in the land would be made up solely of men. In 1981, Justice Sandra Day O'Connor became the first woman to serve on the Supreme Court, receiving 99 votes from the Senate with no opposition. She would go on to redefine the position that 101 men held before her and shape the role for at least four women who have followed in her footsteps.

O'Connor's historic achievement was a reminder that smashing glass ceilings comes with lasting scars. When she attended law school in the 1950s, only two percent of students were women, and they faced blatant ridicule and sexual harassment. Women attempting to break into the male-dominated legal field also faced subtle discrimination in the form of general dismissiveness and unfair hiring practices.

It's no surprise that the daughter of Southwest cattle ranchers had enough grit to fight through this adversity. Born Sandra Day, she grew up without running water or electricity, which made her self-sufficient and resourceful. She moved in with her grandmother so she could attend better schools. She acquired many traits that would prove her to be a qualified and valuable member of the court, often serving as a swing vote on cases involving abortion, affirmative action, and even the disputed 2000 Presidential election.

Decades before joining the Supreme Court, O'Connor took a five-year break from her early career to raise three sons. Sometimes she would cook meals for them using recipes from her Julia Child cookbook (see ch. 49). Other times, she would spend summers away from the boys, who would visit her family at the childhood ranch.

A portrait by artist Danni Dawson hangs on a wall in the lobby near a special exhibit honoring Sandra Day O'Connor as the first woman to serve as a Supreme Court Justice.

Address 1 First Street NE, Washington, DC 20543, +1 (202) 479-3211, www.supremecourt.gov | Getting there Metro to Union Station (Red Line) or Capitol South (Blue, Orange, and Silver Line); bus 30N, 30S, 32, 36 to Independence Avenue & 2nd Street SE | Hours Mon–Fri 9am–4:30pm | Tip *The Four Justices* painting by Nelson Shank at the National Portrait Gallery highlights the first four women to serve on the Supreme Court (8th & G Streets NW, www.npg.si.edu).

51 La Cosecha

A market for Latin American women innovators

Food halls and urban markets are making a comeback in cities across the country. In DC, Union Market District is bringing our city's historic markets back to life with a modern-day market district and dining destination created from the original Center Market from 1871 and the Union Terminal from 1931.

The most recent addition to the neighborhood is La Cosecha, which means "the harvest" in Spanish. La Cosecha is a contemporary market that celebrates Latin American culture with an emphasis on female entrepreneurs and innovators. The space merges art, heritage, culture, and food in a warm and welcoming environment that brings the diversity of Latin American culture under one roof.

A stroll through the market is a truly global journey. Notice the stylish home goods of Zona E, a Colombian boutique owned by mother-and-daughter team Paula Sierra and Luciana Arango. Prepare your tastebuds for the decadent and divinely rich desserts from Arcay Chocolates, founded by Anabella Arcay, a Venezuelan master chocolatier known for creating bonbons and truffles that pair mouth-watering chocolate with flavorful spices, herbs, and fruits. Restaurateur Daniella Senior, who grew up in the Dominican Republic, invites visitors to two bar spaces in the market – Zumo for juice, and Serenata for cocktails. Both spots embody the concept of "Zumo" – the best of what life has to offer.

And if you drop by and smell something frying, it's probably coming from the team at Mosaico Street Food, headed up by Gabriela Febres and Ali Arellano. Both immigrants, the duo is bringing Venezuelan street food to the market, including Latin-style hot dogs. La Cosecha is more than just great food and unique retail spaces. As Gabriela says, "We are excited to be able to show the DC community what it means to be Latino, our culture, food, dance, and the amazing atmosphere we will create."

Address 1280 4th Street NE, Washington, DC 20002, www.lacosechadc.com, lacosecha@edens.com | Getting there Metro to NoMa-Gallaudet (Red Line); bus 90, 92 to Florida Avenue & 3rd Street NE | Hours Tue–Thu & Sun 11am–8pm, Fri & Sat 11am–10pm | Tip Homesick Texans know the best breakfast tacos in the city are from La Tejana. Co-founder Ana-Maria Jaramillo is Colombian-American and uses her experience growing up on both sides of the Texas-Mexico border to create her tasty tacos, available at in-demand pop-ups (www.latejanadc.com).

52 Lady Bird Johnson Park

"Where flowers bloom, so does hope"

Thousands of daffodils and hundreds of tulips bloom every spring, and hardwood trees sport colorful leaves in the fall at Lady Bird Johnson Park, a beloved hidden gem in DC. Formerly known as Columbia Island, the park was created to serve as a symbolic entrance into the capital. It was renamed in 1968 to honor the First Lady who dedicated herself to protecting America's natural beauty.

Claudia Alta Taylor was born in 1912 in Texas and was deemed "purty as a ladybird" by her nursemaid, giving her the famous nickname. She grew up a shy girl who loved the outdoors and took pleasure in exploring the Texas wildflowers. She would graduate from the University of Texas with degrees in history and journalism. She had ambitions of becoming a reporter.

She met Lyndon Baines Johnson shortly after, and it was love at first sight. He proposed on their first date. He was so persistent, she agreed to marry him after just 10 weeks of courting in 1934. She was an extremely important political asset as well, funding LBJ's congressional campaign and running his congressional office during World War II. She was often a mediating force, using her Southern charm to balance out Johnson's rough edges. She was also a shrewd businesswoman, who successfully invested in radio and television, making her the first president's wife to become a millionaire in her own right before becoming First Lady.

As First Lady, she spearheaded a capital city beautification project, oversaw the planting of millions of flowers on National Park Service (NPS) land, and was instrumental in the passage of the Highway Beautification Act, which limited billboards and added trees and flowers along roadways. Her advocacy spanned the rest of her life, including participating in a Women and the Constitution conference in 1988 to assess the document's impact on women. She died in 2007, a living legend with many accolades and awards to her name.

Address Washington Boulevard, Washington, DC 20037, +1 (703) 289-2553, www.nps.gov/gwmp/planyourvisit/ladybirdjohnsonpark.htm | **Getting there** Metro to Arlington Cemetery (Blue Line); by car, take Arlington Memorial Bridge to George Washington Memorial Parkway | **Hours** Daily 6am–10pm | **Tip** Lady Bird Johnson's capital beautification project also created the Floral Library on the National Mall with 93 flower beds and maintained by the NPS (Independence Avenue SW, www.nps.gov/places/000/floral-library-on-the-national-mall.htm).

53 Letelier-Moffitt Memorial
A political assassination, a personal tragedy

On September 21, 1976, Orlando Letelier, an economist, diplomat, and political activist, who had become an outspoken critic of Chilean military dictator Augusto Pinochet, was driving his car around Sheridan Circle, when a bomb exploded. Letelier was not alone in his vehicle but accompanied by his colleague Ronni Karpen Moffitt and her husband of four months, Michael.

Ronni Susan Karpen was born in Passaic, New Jersey and described by her father as "full of life." She majored in education at the University of Maryland, graduated in 1972 and began her career as an elementary school teacher. While she enjoyed teaching, she wanted a career change and started looking for something more meaningful. She became involved with a storefront music center in Adams Morgan, the Music Carry-Out, which lent musical instruments to the community. Ronni played guitar, recorder, flute, and piano, in addition to writing poems and painting. Her work obtaining a grant for the music center connected her to the Institute of Policy Studies (ISP), where she went to work in the fall of 1974.

She met Michael Moffitt while working at ISP, and they married in 1976. Ronni's colleagues described her as sensitive, young, idealistic, hard-working, and friendly, and she had recently been promoted from an assistant to a fund-raiser. She and Michael, both 25 years old, were close colleagues of Orlando Letelier, who had been targeted by the Pinochet regime after the 1973 military coup. The car bomb detonated that day was intended to assassinate Letelier. He died at the scene, and Ronni died at the hospital. Michael survived.

The small memorial that sits here today was unveiled in 1981 in connection with the Letelier-Moffitt Human Rights Award, given annually by the ISP. Every year, a small commemoration ceremony is held to honor the lives of both victims and recognize the ongoing fight to protect human rights.

Address Sheridan Circle NW between Massachusetts Avenue & 23rd Street NW,
Washington, DC 20008, www.ips-dc.org/about/letelier-moffitt-human-rights-awards |
Getting there Metro to Dupont Circle (Red Line); bus N6 to Sheridan Circle &
Massachusetts Avenue NW | Hours Unrestricted | Tip Eleanor Roosevelt, a champion
of human rights, lived nearby with her husband Franklin early in their political careers.
The former Roosevelt home is now the residence of the ambassador of the Republic of Mali
(2131 R Street NW, www.dcwritershomes.wdchumanities.org/eleanor-roosevelt).

54 Letena Restaurant

Yamrot Ezineh serves authentic Ethiopian cuisine

The largest population of Ethiopians outside of Africa is concentrated right here in the greater DC region. Proximity to the country's embassy has earned Washington, DC the reputation as Ethiopia's "second capital." Over several decades of immigration, local neighborhoods have been infused with the culture, and one must-not-miss experience is dining at Letena. Meaning "for health" in Amharic, this Columbia Heights neighborhood restaurant offers authentic Ethiopian food and beverages.

The story of owner Yamrot Ezineh highlights the long-lasting relationship between sister capital cities Washington, DC and Addis Ababa, where she was born. Her approach to food offers a broad range of natural and healthy options. The menu includes both vegetable-forward and hearty meat dishes, like traditional *gulash*, *wot*, and *tibs*. Ezineh emphasizes that these ingredients are readily available because of the strong network in the city. "Everything starts from scratch," she says. This is certainly true for her food, as she returned to Ethiopia to study and research recipes before opening in 2016. But it also speaks to her personal journey.

Ezineh bravely restarted her life's path from scratch several times. She was educated for a career in pharmaceuticals, worked as a chemical engineer, and committed to raising her kids as a homemaker before launching Letena. She credits much of her desire for entrepreneurship to her mother, a banker and self-employed businesswoman, who set a positive example rooted in strength and independence.

Yamrot's family influence is in the foundation of her establishment. After leaving Ethiopia, she spent time in London learning from her relatives who owned a restaurant there. Eventually she met her husband, who is from the DC area, and moved here in 2007. Experiencing the nation's capital must include Ethiopian culture, and Letena is at the top of the list.

Address 3100 14th Street NW, Washington, DC 20010, +1 (202) 733-4830, www.letenadc.com, dine@letenadc.com | Getting there Metro to Columbia Heights (Green and Yellow Line); bus 52, 54 to 14th & Monroe Streets NW | Hours See website | Tip All members of the DC community can join the DC Sister Cities Steering Committee to foster international relationships (os.dc.gov/service/dc-sister-cities).

55 Librarian of Congress

Carla Hayden, the people's librarian

Inscribed upon the walls of the Jefferson Building of the Library of Congress, the oldest federal cultural institution in the country, are the names of great poets, scientists, explorers, and inventors – all men, except the Greek poet Sappho and the Librarian of Congress Carla Hayden. Her name is inscribed with all the past librarians, but her confirmation to this position in 2016 set her apart from the 13 others who have served in this role. Dr. Hayden holds the distinction of not only being the first African American but also the first woman to be the Librarian of Congress, despite the profession being dominated by a female workforce. If the Reading Room had a glass ceiling, Dr. Hayden would certainly have cracked it the moment she was sworn in.

She was also the first Librarian of Congress to establish a Twitter account and has often joked that "librarians are the original search engines." Entering this role during the Age of Technology has made digitizing the materials one of her main priorities as part of her larger plan to make valuable information more accessible to the public. Dr. Hayden has advocated for libraries as vital neighborhood centers that foster education and community. Prior to this position, she was the chief executive officer of the Enoch Pratt Free Library in Baltimore, where she earned a reputation for her bold decisions to keep the library open during civil unrest following a police brutality case involving the death of Freddie Gray in 2015. She acknowledged that the library offered refuge as a safe haven during this extremely emotional and challenging moment.

In 2019, Dr. Hayden appointed Joy Harjo as the 23rd Poet Laureate Consultant in Poetry, the first Native American to serve. Harjo, a member of the Muscogee Creek Nation, was granted a unique extension to serve a third term to complete projects affected by the COVID-19 pandemic.

Address 101 Independence Avenue SE, Washington, DC 20540, +1 (202) 707-8000, www.loc.gov | Getting there Metro to Union Station (Red Line) or Capitol South (Blue, Orange, and Silver Line); bus 30N, 30S, 32, 36 to Independence Avenue & 2nd Street SE | Hours Mon–Sat 8:30am–4:30pm | Tip Stroll through Georgetown past the home of Louise Bogan, the first woman to be honored as US Poet Laureate, originally titled Consultant in Poetry (1207 35th Street NW, www.dcwritershomes.wdchumanities.org/louise-bogan).

56 Lincoln Park
Memorial to Mary McLeod Bethune

The statue of Dr. Mary McLeod Bethune is the only memorial dedicated to an African American woman in any DC public park. The 17-foot bronze statue depicts Bethune's lasting legacy as one of America's most influential educators. Her story has deep roots in Southern culture, from her childhood in South Carolina and down to Florida, where she established the Daytona Literary and Industrial Training School for Negro Girls in 1904, today a co-ed institution renamed Bethune-Cookman University.

Mary McLeod Bethune worked to solve problems by building hospitals in her community, leading anti-lynching campaigns, and hosting registration drives to ensure voters had access to the ballot. She served her nation as a valued advisor to five different presidents, becoming the first African American woman to head a federal agency in 1936 when President Roosevelt appointed her to the Division of Negro Affairs. The statue depicts Bethune holding a cane in her right hand, a unique gift from the Roosevelts, considering she did not physically need a cane, but she enjoyed having it as a conversation starter.

Bethune founded the National Council of Negro Women (NCNW) in 1935 to advocate for and empower women of African descent. She worked closely with Dorothy Height, president of NCNW for over 50 years. Height helped raise approximately $400,000 in funding to erect a memorial statue to Bethune (see ch. 56). Height was present at the memorial's dedication on July 10, 1974, Bethune's 99th birthday.

Bethune's legacy is highlighted in the statue, as she is shown passing along her Last Will and Testament to children of the next generation. The quote on the base reads, "I leave you love, I leave you hope, I leave you a thirst for education, I leave you racial dignity, I leave you a desire to live harmoniously with your fellow man, I leave you, finally, a responsibility to our young people."

Address 1301 East Capitol Street SE, Washington, DC 20003, +1 (202) 690-5185, www.nps.gov/cahi/learn/historyculture/cahi_lincoln.htm | Getting there Metro to Eastern Market (Blue, Orange, and Silver Line); bus 90, 92, 97 to East Capitol & 8th Streets NE, or bus B2 to East Capitol & 15th Streets NE | Hours Unrestricted | Tip Lincoln Park is also home to the Emancipation Memorial, which received its first financial contribution from a formerly enslaved African American woman named Charlotte Scott. She donated her first five dollars earned in freedom to ignite the fundraising campaign (www.nps.gov).

57 The Lockwood DC

Belva Lockwood, a woman of historic firsts

When the staff of this residential apartment building took a field trip to Congressional Cemetery, they were intrigued by the headstone of a woman overlooked by history. Listening to the tour guide share her story inspired the development team to name this new Capitol Hill property after women's rights advocate, Belva Lockwood.

The location matches perfectly with her legacy. The Lockwood DC is just blocks away from where Belva became the first woman lawyer to argue in front of the Supreme Court. You could explore this neighborhood by foot, but it might be more fun to travel around in the same way that the quirky Belva would have: on an adult tricycle with a parrot on her shoulder! It's hard to believe but easy to picture on a visit to the Lockwood DC, where you can view a reimagined portrait by artist Leslie Holt depicting Lockwood and her green bird, or see artist J. J. McCracken's artwork featuring her on her tricycle built to provide functionality for women wearing the traditional long skirts of the time.

A woman riding a bike was scandalous in the 19th century, but Lockwood understood the practicality and advantages of a new technology that offered speedy travel. As her male colleagues riding bikes were more productive in their careers, Lockwood was determined to keep up – and that she did. In 1884, women did not have the right to vote yet, but that didn't prevent Lockwood from becoming the first woman to run an official campaign seeking election as president of the United States.

It's no surprise that the team at the Lockwood DC was so inspired by this woman that they have inscribed her name into their identity. Belva Lockwood was a woman who fought for the rights of the next generation. Artist Kate Hardy closed the gap of time when she included a hidden photo of her young daughter into a ceramic artwork of Lockwood on display in the lobby.

Address 1339 E Street SE, Washington, DC 20003, +1 (833) 340-8434, www.thelockwooddc.com | Getting there Metro to Potomac Avenue (Blue Line); bus 32, 36 to Pennsylvania Avenue & 13th Street SE | Hours See website for lobby hours | Tip Emily Edson Briggs was a pioneering female political journalist, the first president of the Women's National Press Association, and resident of the oldest existing house on Capitol Hill, The Maples (619 D Street SE, https://historicsites.dcpreservation.org/items/show/355).

58 Louise Slaughter Tree

An arboreal tribute to a legislative lioness

There are more than 4,000 trees gracing the grounds of the United States Capitol Complex. The original vision of Frederick Law Olmstead's 1874 landscape plan was to keep the environment natural, with native trees along the walkways and more exotic trees dotted throughout. Among the plantings are memorial and commemorative trees that have been placed to honor important events and people in our history.

An English walnut tree was added to the grounds in April 2018 in honor of Representative Louise Slaughter, a 16-term congresswoman from New York. Slaughter was originally from Kentucky, where she had studied microbiology. She moved to New York and began a career in politics, first in the New York State Assembly and then the US House of Representatives. In Congress, she gained a reputation for being tough, outspoken, and a fierce advocate for women's rights. She was the first woman to chair the powerful House Rules Committee, cementing a legacy as a dynamic leader and a force to be reckoned with.

Her background in science and public health informed her advocacy for women's health legislation. Slaughter secured groundbreaking funding for breast cancer research and fought to ensure that women and minorities are included in all federal health clinical trials. The National Institute of Health awarded Slaughter the "Visionary for Women's Health Research" after Slaughter led the drive to establish an Office of Research on Women's Health within the NIH. She co-authored the Violence Against Women Act and introduced the legislation to establish the Women's Progress Commemorative Commission in 1998 to identify and preserve women's history sites.

Louise Slaughter passed away in March of 2018 at the age of 88, the oldest sitting member of Congress at the time. At the memorial service in Statuary Hall of the United States Capitol Building, Nancy Pelosi said "Louise made the Congress more diverse, more welcoming to women, and more representative of our nation."

Address First Street SE, Washington, DC 20004, www.aoc.gov/tree | Getting there Metro to Capitol South (Blue, Orange, and Silver Line); bus 30N, 30S, 32, 36 to Independence & New Jersey Avenues SE | Hours Unrestricted | Tip Networking in DC can be a drag, which is why Netwalking founder Jessica Tunon took movers and shakers out of conference rooms and bars and developed a program that blends walking for fitness with fostering meaningful connections (www.netwalkglobal.com).

59_Lucretia Mott Portrait
A Quaker activist at the National Portrait Gallery

"Let woman then go on, not asking favors, but claiming as a right the removal of all hindrances to her elevation in the scale of being." – Lucretia Mott, social reformer

The National Portrait Gallery was established in 1962 as a museum to display portraiture of "men and women who have made significant contributions to the history, development, and culture of the people of the United States." Among the busts and portraits of notable women who shaped and led this nation is a figure whose name and contributions are often overshadowed by her contemporaries: Lucretia Coffin Mott.

Born in 1793 in Massachusetts, Lucretia received an unusual education for a young woman. She studied at the liberal Nine Partners School, run by the Society of Friends, or Quakers, which would become a cornerstone for the rest of her life. The Quaker faith, rooted in an egalitarian idea of faith, would be a welcoming space for women and often overlap with progressive movements like abolition and suffrage.

Lucretia was passionate about abolition. She refused to use goods produced with slave labor and eventually became a Quaker minister, traveling to deliver anti-slavery sermons. Her husband, James Mott, was a founding member of the American Anti-Slavery Society, and Lucretia was the only woman to speak at the organizing meeting. She opened her home to enslaved people escaping to freedom.

She attended the General Anti-Slavery Convention in London in 1840, where she would meet Elizabeth Cady Stanton. They became close friends and allies, seeing parallels between the fight to end slavery and the fight for women's rights. Mott helped form the American Equal Rights Association, serving as its first president, and she helped organize the Seneca Falls Convention in 1848. Mott often avoided party politics, driven by a moral obligation for equality, but she dedicated the remainder of her life to suffrage.

Address 8th & G Streets NW, Washington, DC 20001, +1 (202) 633-8300, www.npg.si.edu | **Getting there** Metro to Gallery Place-Chinatown (Green and Yellow Line); bus 70, 74 to 7th & G Streets NW | **Hours** See website | **Tip** Lucretia Mott is honored, along with Susan B. Anthony and Elizabeth Cady Stanton, in *Portrait Monument* by Adelaide Johnson in the rotunda of the United States Capitol Building. Contact your local congressperson to request a tour (First Street NE, www.visitthecapitol.gov).

60 Martin's Tavern Booth 3

Where Jacqueline went from Bouvier to Kennedy

Jacqueline Lee Bouvier was born into wealth, status, and sophistication – ideals she would embody her entire life. In her senior yearbook, she was celebrated for "her wit, her accomplishment as a horsewoman, and her unwillingness to become a housewife." She was destined for adventure, spending her time abroad in college and traveling around Europe with her sister Lee after graduation, the subject of her only autobiography.

Jackie had ambitions for a career in publishing and landed a prestigious editorship at *Vogue* magazine, only to quit on her first day based on the advice of the managing editor, who told her to get serious about her marriage prospects. She moved to DC to start work at the *Washington Times-Herald.* Entering as a secretary, she was promoted to the paper's "Inquiring Camera Girl." She would photograph people on the street while posing unique questions and publishing their quotes.

In May 1952, Jackie attended a dinner party in Georgetown and was introduced to Representative John F. Kennedy. There was an immediate attraction, and the two grew serious. One of their regular spots to dine was Martin's Tavern, a Georgetown stalwart opened in 1933. Kennedy won a Senate seat in 1952 and set his eye on marriage. The following year, the couple was sitting in their regular booth, number three, when John asked Jackie to consider a proposal.

Jackie waited to accept JFK's offer until after her next assignment covering the coronation of the young Queen Elizabeth II. She spent a month in London as a journalist, documenting the landmark event. It was not until she returned and met Kennedy at Martin's that she accepted his marriage proposal. Their engagement was announced publicly on June 25, 1953.

The restaurant is run today by its first woman, the founder's great-great granddaughter Lauren, and you can sit in the Proposal Booth, a favorite tradition for couples.

The Proposal Booth

JFK and Jackie frequently dined in Booth 3 at Martin's Tavern to be lured just 2 blocks from the Tavern.

Address 1264 Wisconsin Avenue NW, Washington, DC 20007, +1 (202) 333-7370, www.martinstavern.com, info@martinstavern.com | Getting there Bus 30N, 30S, 31, 33 to Wisconsin Avenue NW & N Street NW | Hours Mon–Fri 11am–11:30pm, Sat 10am–10:30pm, Sun 9am–11:30pm | Tip Georgetown was home to the Kennedys for a decade. Go see the brick house with green shutters that Jackie and John shared from 1957 until they moved into the White House in January 1961 (3307 N Street NW, www.georgetowndc.com/guide/self-guided-kennedy-walking-tour).

61 Mary Ann Shadd Cary

First Black female publisher in North America

The story of marginalized groups is often told through oral history because of the limited resources available for more formal record keeping. With laws and policies in place to restrict reading, writing, and expression, the most vulnerable groups in society have often had to rely on verbal storytelling to share their experiences.

Mary Ann Shadd Cary most likely understood these obstacles as she used the power of the written word to infiltrate systems of oppression. Not only was she the first Black female publisher and editor in North America, she was also a revolutionary woman whose intersectional approach to activism challenged the status quo.

She studied at a Pennsylvania Quaker school as a child and embraced egalitarian causes like abolition and women's rights. The Shadd family hosted a stop on the Underground Railroad until Congress passed the Fugitive Slave Act in 1850. They emigrated to Canada, where Mary Ann Shadd ran her anti-slavery newspaper and married Thomas Cary. She returned to the US to work as an Army recruiting officer during the Civil War, enlisting Black soldiers for the Union. After the war, she worked as a DC public school teacher while studying law. She became the first Black woman to enroll in the Howard University School of Law.

Mary Ann Shadd Cary was a member of the National Woman Suffrage Association and signed the Declaration of the Rights of Women. She presented herself to the DC Board of Registration on April 14, 1871 to provide proof of age and residence in DC so that her name would be added as a registered voter. Days after the board rejected her request, she documented the wrongful decision by having it sworn on paper by a public notary. The plaque outside the house she lived in between 1881 and 1886 designates the building as a National Historic Landmark and recognizes Mary Ann Shadd Cary as a "Renaissance Woman."

Address 1421 W Street NW, Washington, DC 20009, www.nps.gov/places/the-mary-ann-shadd-cary-house.htm | Getting there Metro to U Street (Green and Yellow Line); bus 52, 54 to 14th Street & Florida Avenue NW | Hours Unrestricted from outside only | Tip The Rita Bright Family and Youth Center is named for a Columbia Heights neighborhood organizer, alumni of American University, and co-founder of the Community of Hope Church (2500 14th Street NW, www.dpr.dc.gov/page/rita-bright-community-center-01).

62 Mary Livingston Ripley Garden

Mary Livingston Ripley's fragrant oasis

At the Mary Livingston Ripley Garden, in the heart of one of the busiest spots in DC, the air is fragrant and aromatic. A quiet oasis in the middle of the National Mall, this unusual, curvilinear garden provides a half-acre of space for reflection and solitude surrounded by seasonal plants and hanging baskets.

The garden was the passion project of Mary Livingston Ripley, a lifelong horticulturist, photographer, entomologist, and gardener. Born to a prestigious New York family, Mary Livingston served her country as a clerk for the Office of Strategic Services in World War II. While traveling with the OSS (the precursor to the modern-day CIA), Livingston was roommates with Julia McWilliams, who later became famous as Julia Child (see ch. 49). Livingston would meet Dillon Ripley while stationed in Sri Lanka and marry the man who would become the eighth secretary of the Smithsonian Institution.

Mary was deeply involved in the Smithsonian, founding the Smithsonian Women's Committee in 1966. She frequently accompanied her husband on scientific expeditions, documenting their travels with her camera, searching for insects, and even performing taxidermy. In 1978, she persuaded the Smithsonian to convert a patch of land alongside the Arts and Industries Building, slated to become a parking lot, into a fragrant garden for Smithsonian employees and visitors alike. To help green the Smithsonian's garden in its early years, Mary had plants transferred from her home gardens in Connecticut.

Today, the garden is designed to attract birds, bees, and butterflies, as well as people, drawn by the sweet smells of blossoms. In 1988, the Women's Committee added a plaque honoring Ripley, "their founder and friend." Look for it on the brick flower bed facing Jefferson Drive garden entrance.

MARY LIVINGSTON RIPLEY
Garden

Smithsonian Institution

May 25, 1988

This garden was created by the
Smithsonian Institution Women's Committee
to honor their founder and friend.

Address 850 Jefferson Drive SW, Washington, DC 20560, +1 (202) 633-2220, www.gardens.si.
edu/gardens/ripley-garden, gardens@si.edu | Getting there Metro to Smithsonian (Blue, Orange,
and Silver Line); bus 16C, 74 to Independence Avenue & 7th Street SW; DC Circulator
to Jefferson Drive & 7th Street SW | Hours Unrestricted | Tip Explore another kind of garden
at the National Gallery of Art Sculpture Garden – look for Louise Bourgeois' oversized bronze
spider (7th Street & Constitution Avenue NW, www.nga.gov/visit/sculpture-garden.html).

63 Maya Angelou Stairs

"When I decided to speak, I had a lot to say."

"I have never seen Maya Angelou speechless," said actress Cicely Tyson when she eulogized her beloved friend in 2014. The passing of Dr. Angelou was a great loss, as her words left a vibration for generations to feel. Her voice was her legacy, but long before she recited poetry at the 1993 Presidential Inauguration, Angelou spent five years of her childhood completely and voluntarily mute.

Born Marguerite Johnson, she was reprimanded for speaking up against injustice and convinced that her voice had killed people, so she thought "it was better not to speak." At seven years old, she committed her most formative years to reading every book in the Black school library. When she received second-hand books that didn't have covers from the white school, she fixed them up, using shingles and lace…then she read and memorized them all, from William Shakespeare to Langston Hughes.

Angelou was challenged by a teacher, who told her that she would never like poetry until she spoke it – that she needed to feel how it rolls across her tongue, "over her teeth, and through her lips." She found a quiet space under her Alabama house, near the chickens, and began speaking her poetry. Dr. Angelou reflected and said, "When I decided to speak, I had a lot to say." And that she did, sharing these stories directly in an award-winning documentary, *Maya Angelou: And Still I Rise*.

The story about how these cast-iron stairs landed in front of a house on a quaint neighborhood street is a mystery. But the site of Maya Angelou's poem "Alone" offers a sense of identity and belonging for those who take the time to notice the stairs with curiosity and intention. *Lying, thinking / Last night / How to find my soul a home / Where water is not thirsty / And bread loaf is not stone / I came up with one thing / And I don't believe I'm wrong / That nobody / But nobody / Can make it out here alone.*

Address 1015 P Street NW, Washington, DC 20001, www.mayaangeloufilm.com | Getting there Metro to U Street (Green and Yellow Line); bus 64, G2, G8 to P & 11th Streets NW | Hours Unrestricted from the outside only | Tip Look for *Nourishing and Flourishing with Delight*, a colorful mural by artist Eric Rickis featuring a portrait of the writer, on the exterior of the Maya Angelou Public Charter School (5600 East Capitol Street NE, www.muralsdcproject.com).

Lying, thinking, last night how to find my soul a home

Where water is not thirsty and bread loaf is not stone

I came up with one thing and I don't believe I'm wrong

That nobody, but nobody can make it out here alone.

From "Alone" by Maya Angelou

64 Maydān

Rose Previte creates a gathering place

She was 18 years old when she embarked on a solo trip to Washington, DC. Stepping off that Amtrak train, she admired the beauty of historic Union Station for the first time. That moment is etched in the memory of Rose Previte, who grew up in rural Ohio, traveled the world, and settled in the nation's capital.

After traveling to Russia, Previte found inspiration to open a restaurant she'd call Compass Rose. While working through the tedious process of securing investments and a location for her new venture, she paused for a short wellness journey to an ashram in New York, where she meditated for three days. With renewed energy, she returned to Washington, DC, where she happened to connect deeply with the first building she scouted. The self-professed history nerd appreciated the 130-year-old structure, as well as the upstairs apartment where she desired to live, just as her dad's family had lived above their Italian grocery store in New Jersey.

Rose earned a master's degree in Public Policy from George Mason University and managed the business' complex licensing herself. While researching at the DC Public Library, a moment of synergy came when she discovered that the original 1887 permit for her future restaurant was dated the same as her birthday. Soon after, Compass Rose was established, with repurposed decor and a menu based on international cuisines inspired by Rose and her husband's travels.

Her next restaurant, Maydān, would pay homage to her Lebanese mother, grandmother, and aunts, who taught her how to cook. Maydān serves Middle Eastern cuisine prepared on an open fire. Previte trained her chefs to cook authentic food by sending them on a trip through five countries. Their teachers? Grandmothers with years of wisdom and family traditions to pass on. Maydān is not just a restaurant – it is a memorial honoring generations of women from Morocco, Tunisia, Turkey, Georgia, and Lebanon.

Address 1346 Florida Avenue NW, Washington, DC 20009, +1 (202) 885-9848, www.maydandc.com, meet@maydandc.com | **Getting there** Metro to U Street (Green and Yellow Line); DC Circulator to 14th & U Streets NW | **Hours** See website | **Tip** The Whitelaw Hotel was a social center for the Black community listed in the *Green Book* during segregation. Many prominent entertainers stayed here, but the service staff lived in apartments across the Street, the same building that would become Compass Rose (1839 13th Street NW, https://historicsites.dcpreservation.org/items/show/59).

65 Miss Pixie's

Pixie Windsor stacks it deep and sells it cheap

It's one of those places that curious minds just can't seem to pass by without stopping in to explore. The bright pink exterior of Miss Pixie's is just as inviting as the shop itself, which is full of "furnishings and whatnot." You may start out empty-handed strolling down 14th Street, but you'll easily leave this shop carrying bags full of tchotchkes or requesting an UberXL to haul away a newly purchased Shenandoah table.

There is something new to discover around every corner, begging the question, "Do I need this or do I want this?" The answer is always, "Yes!" The groovy vibe matched with the vintage products is a feel-good experience for folks looking to furnish their condos entirely or just add some funky flair. How did these odds and ends land in the middle of DC's urban neighborhood of Logan Circle? All aisles lead to the creative energy of Pixie Windsor, owner and vintage furniture connoisseur.

She walked into a neighborhood shop one day and learned that it would be closing. Windsor jumped at the opportunity to take it over and turned her love of auctions, yard sales, and antiques into a business in 1997. She eventually outgrew that Adams Morgan location and moved into the current spot in 2008, which was previously Powell Auto Parts. The original concept was supposed to include a bar and eatery inside, but at some point, those plans fell away, and Pixie moved on her business plan to "stack it deep and sell it cheap." She expected to stay here for two years – that was over a decade ago.

Behind the counter, Windsor proudly displays the personality and values of her business. Framed and hanging are accolades such as "Best Vintage Store" and "Best of Gay DC" – next to a sign that reads, *If you are grouchy, irritable, or just plain mean, there will be a $10 charge for putting up with you.* There's no haggling here, but enjoy your signature pink pen that comes with every purchase.

Address 1626 14th Street NW, Washington, DC 20009, +1 (202) 232-8171, www.misspixies.com,
pixie@misspixies.com | Getting there Metro to U Street (Green and Yellow Line); bus 52 to
14th & R Streets NW | Hours Daily 11am–6pm | Tip Gina Schaefer founded Logan Hardware
in 2003, part of a wave of redevelopment in Logan Circle. She's grown the business into
13 hardware stores that employ over 300 people, all centered around the idea of shopping
and buying local (1734 14th Street NW, www.acehardwaredc.com).

66 Missing Soldiers Office
Clara Barton, angel of the battlefield

In 1996, Richard Lyons, an employee of the General Services Administration (GSA), was doing a routine inspection of a building slated for demolition. On the third floor, Richard felt something – or someone – tap him on the shoulder. He turned to see a single envelope hanging down from the ceiling, where he discovered a stockpile of artifacts, including a sign that read *Missing Soldiers Office, 3rd Story, Room 9, Miss Clara Barton*. Today, it's a museum dedicated to Barton's life and legacy.

Clarissa Harlowe Barton was one of the first female federal employees. She risked her life to bring much-needed supplies and support to the men fighting in the Civil War. She went on to found the American Red Cross (see ch. 90). She dedicated her life to serving others and breaking glass ceilings (see ch. 43).

Clara was working at the US Patent Office in DC when the Civil War broke out. She learned that troops stationed in the capital needed supplies, so she began to gather and distribute them. She eventually convinced the government to give her battlefield passes so she could bring medical supplies and moral support to the front, where she was called an "Angel of the Battlefield."

The personal connections she made with the soldiers became invaluable when families began seeking information regarding their missing soldiers after the war. Barton asked President Abraham Lincoln to grant her an appointment as a general correspondent to reply to families' inquiries. In 1865, she published the first "Roll of Missing Men." She also went to Andersonville to identify graves and notify families. She spent the next three years compiling information from soldiers about their comrades and updating her rolls. In her final report to Congress in 1868, she noted that her office had handled 63,182 inquiries, written 41,855 letters, mailed 58,693 circulars, distributed 99,057 copies of her rolls, and identified 22,000 men.

Address 437 7th Street NW, Washington, DC 20004, +1 (202) 824-0613, www.clarabartonmuseum.org, info@civilwarmed.org | Getting there Metro to Gallery Place-Chinatown (Green, Red, and Yellow Line); bus D6, 70, 74 to E & 7th Streets NW | Hours See website | Tip President Lincoln's NW cottage provides incredible insight into the experiences of Lincoln, First Lady Mary Todd Lincoln, and their family during the Civil War (140 Rock Creek Church Road NW, www.lincolncottage.org).

67 Myrtilla Miner's Legacy

The education pioneer who founded UDC

A woman named Myrtilla Miner founded the "Normal School for Colored Girls" in 1851. Over time, the institution merged several times until 1976, when it was established as The University of the District of Columbia (UDC).

Miner's idea to educate African American girls in a racially segregated, pre-Civil War Washington was met with great resistance. Frederick Douglass expressed his doubt in a letter reflecting back to when he met Miner, a white abolitionist. He wrote, "Here, I thought, is another enterprise, wild, dangerous, desperate, and impractical, destined only to bring failure and suffering." While Douglass rightfully cautioned of the hostile public sentiment of the city, Miner persisted nevertheless.

One of her biggest challenges was fundraising. She would accept an initial $100 from Reverend Henry Ward Beecher, a philanthropic Quaker whose cousin Harriet Beecher Stowe would also donate $1,000 of royalties from her book, *Uncle Tom's Cabin*. Once the "Normal School for Colored Girls" was operational, Miner and her students were targets of violence. Bigots would insult the girls entering school, throw stones, and even tried to set the schoolhouse on fire. Miner became friendly with the Edmonson family (see ch. 10), who would teach Myrtilla and their daughter Emily how to shoot a pistol.

Myrtilla Miner was one of the most influential educators in DC, known for developing programs that train teachers and has an elementary school named for her today. Frederick Douglass wrote about her 30 years later: "I marvel all the more at the thought, the zeal, the faith, and the courage of Myrtilla Miner in daring to be the pioneer of such a movement for education here, in the District of Columbia, the very citadel of slavery, the place most zealously watched and guarded by the slave power, and where humane tendencies were most speedily detected and sternly opposed."

Address 4200 Connecticut Avenue NW, Washington, DC 20008, +1 (202-274-5000, www.udc.edu | Getting there Metro to Van Ness-UDC (Red Line); bus L2 to Connecticut Avenue & Veazey Terrace NW | Hours See website for classes and events | Tip The National Training School for Women and Girls was founded in 1909 by Nannie Helen Burroughs to teach independent women about Godliness, cleanliness, housekeeping, printing, dressmaking, and entrepreneurship (50th Street & Nannie Helen Burroughs Avenue NE, www.culturaltourismdc.org/portal/820).

68 National Capitol Columns
Remembering two pillars of preservation

The United States National Arboretum is one of DC's most photographic sites, hidden in the urban landscape of the city's Northeast quadrant. One of the most obscure attractions in this 446-acre nature preserve is the National Capitol Columns, 22 Corinthian-style pillars standing freely in the east Ellipse field. Most visitors look up in awe as they admire the larger-than-life columns, but few realize that women's history is at their feet, both figuratively and literally.

Originally part of the United States Capitol Building in 1828, the columns were removed when the oversized cast-iron dome was added. A benefactress of the Arboretum named Ethel Garrett began a campaign to preserve and highlight the columns in a public setting after they'd spent decades in storage. She called upon her friend and landscape designer Russell Page to assist with finding a location. Unfortunately, Garrett passed away before seeing her vision come to fruition in 1990.

The stones below the iconic Capitol columns are engraved with honorary messages and acknowledgements. Look for the one placed in memory of Phoebe Apperson Hearst and her husband Senator George Hearst. Phoebe came from simple beginnings in Missouri but would inherit her husband's wealth as a widow. Much like Ethel Garrett, Phoebe Hearst worked to preserve history. As a 29-year member of the Mount Vernon Ladies Association, she served as second vice regent in an effort to preserve George and Martha Washington's historic home. Hearst contributed to the renovation of Mount Vernon's seawall along the Potomac River and financed the estate's first electrical system and telephone in the 1890s.

Records also show that she purchased a sack-back Windsor chair from the granddaughter of Christopher Shields, an enslaved man who served as George Washington's personal valet. The chair had been in the room where Washington died.

Address 3501 New York Avenue NE, Washington, DC 20002, +1 (202) 245-4523, www.usna.usda.gov | Getting there Metro to Stadium Armory (Blue and Orange Line); bus B2 to Bladensburg Road & Rand Place NE | Hours Daily 8am–5pm | Tip Mount Olivet Cemetery is the final resting place of Mary Surratt, the first woman to be executed by the United States Government for her involvement in the assassination of President Lincoln (see ch. 93) (1300 Bladensburg Road NE, www.ccaw.org).

69__NGA Impressionists
Mary Cassatt makes a strong impression

In 1937, Congress accepted a gift from banker Andrew W. Mellon: a collection of valuable artworks and the funds necessary to build a new museum. And so the National Gallery of Art (NGA) was born. The museum's holdings have grown to encompass an encyclopedic journey through the world of art. One of the highlights is its collection of Impressionist art, including almost 300 works by a woman who would help define the genre.

Impressionism was a progressive art movement with its egalitarian inclusion of women in the organization, promotion, and creation of its exhibitions. The "Group of Independent Artists" first appeared together in 1874, and Mary Cassatt was invited to join shortly after. Cassatt spent five years in Europe in her youth. She was exposed to the work of great artists and knew she was meant to join them.

She began her training at the Pennsylvania Academy of Fine Arts but grew frustrated by the patronizing attitude of her male instructors and the restrictions placed on female students, such as not being allowed to work with live models. She instead moved to Paris in 1866. The next 10 years were a struggle, as Cassatt fought against the ingrained sexism of the art world. When Edgar Degas invited her to show her work with the Impressionists at their independent shows, she became the second female artist to join the group, after Berthe Morisot. She learned new techniques and found that her work blossomed under Degas' influence.

Cassatt's representations of women gave depth to her subjects, often hinted at meaningful inner lives, and reflected the New Woman of the era. She was an outspoken advocate for women's equality and suffrage. She never married for fear it would conflict with her career. She served as an advisor to major art collectors, guiding them to support Impressionism and modern art – and to add female artists to their collections.

Address 6th Street & Constitution Avenue NW, Washington, DC 20565, +1 (202) 712-7451, www.nga.gov | Getting there Metro to Archives-Navy Memorial-Penn Quarter (Green and Yellow Line); bus 70, 74, 335, 345, P6 to 7th Street & Constitution Avenue NW | Hours See website and exhibitions | Tip You can explore more modern art at the Phillips Collection, including works by Berthe Morisot, Georgia O'Keeffe, and Berenice Abbott (1600 21st Street NW, www.phillipscollection.org).

70 Nuns of the Battlefield

A monument to Civil War angels of mercy

Prior to the Civil War, there were few professional women in the world of medicine, with the exception of nuns from Catholic orders. Nuns were pioneers in bringing women into medicine, as they ran hospitals and other sites for the sick and injured. As the war ripped the nation apart and thrust our country into a bloody conflict, over 600 Catholic nurses answered the call of duty and rushed to serve the ill and fallen soldiers.

The *Nuns of the Battlefield* monument was the brainchild of Ellen Ryan Jolly, president of the women's auxiliary branch of the Ancient Order of Hibernians, a prominent Irish Catholic organization. Jolly had grown up hearing stories of the nuns who had served during the war and set her sights on building a memorial to honor them. Her initial request was denied by the War Department, so she spent 10 years compiling evidence to prove the service and deepest commitment of these women.

Jolly uncovered documents, including letters to President Lincoln from members of his staff attesting to the nuns' service and newspaper articles highlighting the work of various orders, to convince Congress to approve a Civil War Nurses Memorial. She also spearheaded efforts to raise the $50,000 necessary for construction. Irish artist Jerome Conner was selected to design the structure. It was dedicated in 1924, with Sister Magdalene of the Sisters of Mercy, who had served as a nurse during the war, in attendance.

Conner's sculpture depicts 12 nuns wearing a diverse set of habits, representing various orders that provided care during the war. Seated angels flank the memorial, representing Peace and Patriotism. The inscription pays tribute to the nursing and palliative care provided by the nuns. It reads, *To the memory and in honor of The Various Orders of Sisters who gave their services as nurses on the battlefield and in hospitals during the Civil War.*

Address 1745 M Street NW, Washington, DC 20036, www.ncpc.gov/memorials/detail/85 | Getting there Metro to Dupont Circle (Red Line); bus 42, 43, L2, N6 to Connecticut Avenue & M Street NW | Hours Unrestricted | Tip Dupont Circle was home to Catholic writer Frances Parkinson Keyes, who wrote about her life as a senator's wife. She lived in the Anchorage building in Dupont Circle, a popular residence for politicos (1900 Q Street NW, www.dcwritershomes.wdchumanities.org).

71 Octagon House

The haunted house that helped build a capital

In Foggy Bottom you'll find an unusually shaped structure with a rich history steeped in spooky rumors. The Octagon House, completed around 1800, was designed by Dr. William Thornton, best known for designing the United States Capitol Building. The house was built for Colonel John Tayloe, a wealthy Virginia planter, at the suggestion of George Washington, who was hoping to grow the federal city. The irregular size of the lot forced Thornton to create the building's unique octagon shape.

When the British occupied Washington in August 1814 and burned the city's federal buildings, including the White House, Tayloe offered his home to President and First Lady Madison (see ch. 19) as a temporary residence. For six months, while President Madison made his office in the upstairs study, Dolley Madison used her legendary hostess skills to bring the city to life after the burning of Washington. The Tayloe home would later host a girls' school, US Navy office space, and apartment-style housing. The American Institute of Architects (AIA), the current owners, acquired the building in 1898, using it as their headquarters before converting it into a historic home museum in 1970.

While visitors are curious about the house's history, many are drawn by the tales of hauntings. Dolley Madison is a frequently spotted spirit, often accompanied by the smell of lilacs. A group of ghost hunters in 1888 stayed overnight and reported hearing screams of unseen women throughout the night. The most notorious – and least authenticated – legend says that two of Colonel Tayloe's daughters died in the same way in the house, just a few years apart. Both daughters were alleged to have fallen to their deaths from the upper landings after quarreling with their father over their choice of husbands. The ghosts of the young women have been seen crumpled at the bottom of the stairs or leaning over the upper railings.

Address 1799 New York Avenue NW, Washington, DC 20006, +1 (202) 626-7439, www.architectsfoundation.org/octagon-museum, octagon@architectsfoundation.org | Getting there Metro to Farragut West (Blue, Orange, and Silver Line); bus 7Y, 80 to 18th & F Streets NW | Hours Thu–Sat 1–4pm | Tip The National Building Museum is dedicated to architecture, design, and engineering. Chloethiel Woodard Smith, a pioneering female architect, was a founding trustee (401 F Street NW, www.nbm.org).

72   Olive Seward Statue
The strange story of a mysterious statue

Wandering the streets of historic Eastern Market, one might expect to come across a quaint bookstore or an idyllic park, not the statue of an idealized Victorian lady, gazing woefully from the front yard of a private home towards a park named for former Secretary of State William Seward. The statue of Olive Risley Seward has puzzled residents and visitors alike for decades.

Shortly following the attack on his life on April 14, 1865, William Seward lost both his wife and only daughter. He found himself without any female companionship when the daughter of a friend caught his eye – Olive Risley. Olive would become his closest platonic confidant and traveling companion. As Olive was more than 30 years younger than Seward, gossip naturally ensued. So, to preserve Olive's reputation, Seward would adopt her in 1870, even though her father was still alive and well.

Olive's travels with Seward sparked in her a love of writing that she would embrace throughout her lifetime. She was credited as the editor of Seward's book *Travels Around the World*, which was published after his death and would go on to be a bestseller. Olive was noted for hosting a bohemian literary salon and would publish her own series of *Around the World Stories* based on her own travels. In 1874, she founded the Literary Society of Washington, unusual for its inclusion of women as members from the beginning. One of her co-founders, Sara Carr Upton, also a writer, would go on to be her lifelong companion and executor of her estate.

In the 1970s, artist John Cavanaugh felt that Seward Square needed a statue of some kind to complete it. He set to work creating a statue of Olive out of hammered lead over burlap. Having no pictures of her to work from, he simply created her in the image of the perfect Victorian woman. She is positioned so that she is forever gazing towards the park bearing the name of her adopted father.

Address 601 North Carolina Avenue SE, Washington, DC 20003, www.dcwritershomes.
wdchumanities.org/david-kresh | **Getting there** Metro to Eastern Market (Blue, Orange,
and Silver Line); bus 30N, 30S, 32, 36 to Pennsylvania Avenue & 6th Street SE | **Hours**
Unrestricted | **Tip** Just around the corner is Capitol Hill favorite Labyrinth Games & Puzzles.
Owner Kathleen Donahue stocks over 3,000 games geared towards all ages and interests
(645 Pennsylvania Avenue SE, www.labyrinthgameshop.com).

73 — The Outrage
Rebecca Lee Funk creates a hub for activism

She received the keys on January 1, 2017, and would have only days to design and convert the space into the official pop-up shop for the Women's March. This challenge became more difficult once The Outrage founder Rebecca Lee Funk learned that she was pregnant – on New Year's Eve, just 11 hours before she unlocked the door to her first brick and mortar location.

The early days were eventful, as crowds formed outside the store to purchase feminist apparel, like "Nasty Women Unite" buttons and "The Future is Female" t-shirts. The customers became friends while waiting in line, sharing stories and exchanging hugs – as women often do in lines and restrooms. Like a game of 1990s' telephone, news had passed through the line of Funk's pregnancy, and random women began to deliver her ginger ale and saltines for nausea. After baby Leo was born, Funk carried him on her hip to work events, where her feminist community would collectively help care for him.

Before all the media and press, Funk's business started as an e-commerce store that she had built from her laptop in the DC Public Library and local coffee shops. She was an economist in her previous career, and though she has a strong love for calculus, she decided that she would quit her job to focus on growing the business. She supported herself by working as a bartender at Nationals Park, and with unrelenting discipline and even a bit of obsession, Funk gave birth to The Outrage.

The brand maintained their activism efforts beyond the Women's March by officially partnering with major movements like March for Our Lives, Families Belong Together, and March for Science. The shop on 14th Street expanded into a new location, with an event space for community gatherings. The Outrage continues to make a donation with every single purchase to connect their customers with progressive causes they care about.

Address 1811 14th Street NW, Washington, DC 20009, +1 (202) 885-9848, www.the-outrage.com | Getting there Metro to U Street (Green and Yellow Line); DC Circulator to 14th & P Streets NW | Hours Daily noon–6pm | Tip Before the 2017 Women's March, there was the 1913 Suffrage Parade, when activists protested against President Wilson the day before his inauguration. An image of these first wave feminists stretches across the lobby of the JW Marriott Hotel (1331 Pennsylvania Avenue NW, www.jw-marriott.marriott.com).

74 Patterson Mansion

Journalist, publisher, and ultimate insider

Standing in Dupont Circle today is a mansion that harkens back to the Gilded Age, when the neighborhood was a distant enclave for the richest residents of DC: the Patterson Mansion. The neoclassical structure, completed in 1903, would become the home of Eleanor Josephine Medill "Cissy" Patterson.

Cissy was described as a leading light of DC society and was dubbed as one of the "Three Graces" along with her peers Alice Roosevelt and Marguerite Cassini. It shocked the city when, at age 22, she secretly wed a Polish Count she had met while traveling. She went to live with him at his manor in Russian Poland, but things turned sour. They separated multiple times before Cissy determined she had to leave. But her escape was stopped when her husband tracked her down and kidnapped their only daughter. It would ultimately take 13 years and the intervention of the US State Department for Cissy to obtain a divorce and return to the United States.

Once back in DC, Cissy pursued a career in journalism. She wrote for the *New York Daily News* before becoming the editor of the *Washington Herald* and the *Washington Times*, both owned by William Randolph Hearst (see ch. 68). She made both papers a success by investing in society reporting, hiring women as reporters, and giving new visual style to the previously staid papers. She also wrote about her private life, publishing two thinly-veiled novels about her "frenemy" Alice Roosevelt (see ch. 3).

In 1939, Cissy was able to purchase both newspapers from Hearst and combined them into a single paper, the *Washington Times-Herald,* one of the leading papers in the nation's capital. Cissy was a pioneer for women in publishing and journalism, even facing espionage charges for publishing intelligence information during World War II. The charges were dropped when it became clear the Navy censors had approved the story before publishing.

Address 15 Dupont Circle NW, Washington, DC 20036, www.pattersonmansion.com |
Getting there Metro to Dupont Circle (Red Line); bus G2, N6 to P & 18th Streets NW |
Hours Viewable from the outside only | Tip One of the best salons in Dupont Circle is
Brown Beauty Co-op, founded in 2018 by Kimberly Smith and Amaya Smith (best friends
but not related) as a sanctuary for women of color to shop for beauty products, network, and
find community (1365 Connecticut Avenue NW, Suite 100, www.brownbeautyco-op.com).

75 Pennsylvania Avenue

Remember the ladies in the blueprint of America

America's Main Street paints women's history in the District with a broad stroke of perspective. From scandalous rendezvous points to formal pageantry and historic preservation, Washington women have shaped the nation's capital in the most revolutionary ways.

The first woman to live at 1600 Pennsylvania Avenue was First Lady Abigail Adams, whose feminist advice to her husband cautioned the Founding Fathers to "Remember the ladies." She was the first, but certainly not the last, woman to help steer the country from inside the White House.

Some "ladies of the night" influenced politics a bit more discreetly by sharing personal time and attention with the government's most notorious elected officials. Long before food trucks lined the National Mall, Downtown DC was a promiscuous Red Light District known as Hooker's Division, with more than 50 saloons and 109 "bawdy-houses." Commonly operating these brothel businesses were madams, such as Mary Ann Hall, who died in 1886 with an estate worth nearly two million dollars in modern currency.

Women continued to claim Pennsylvania Avenue as a space of their own throughout the twentieth century. Feminists in 1913 organized one of the most extravagant civil rights marches of all time and they would return over the decades wearing green ERA pins and pink crocheted hats. Some women's history downtown has faded, but one significant building remains as a testament to women's creativity and conviction.

The Old Post Office complex was renamed the Nancy Hanks Center in 1986 to honor a woman who fought to preserve the building. As chair of the National Endowment of the Arts (1969–1977), Hanks was joined by the local group Don't Tear It Down to safeguard the structure from demolition. She lived by her "conviction that the cornerstone of any culture is the nurtured talent of its creative artists."

Address Pennsylvania Avenue between 4th & 15th Streets NW, Washington, DC 20565, www.culturaltourismdc.org/portal/822 | Getting there Metro to Archives-Navy Memorial (Green and Yellow Line) or Federal Triangle (Blue, Orange, and Silver Line) | Hours Unrestricted | Tip The White House Visitor Center showcases the history of those who have called The White House home and includes a stirring video, narrated by several former Presidents, First Ladies, and First Children (1450 Pennsylvania Avenue NW, www.nps.gov/whho/planyourvisit/white-house-visitor-center.htm).

76_Phyllis Wheatley YWCA
The hill she climbed, a revolutionary journey

A seven-year-old girl from West Africa was one of 75 people to survive an eight-week journey to the British North American colonies on a slave ship called the *Phillis*. After these people were traded in 1761 for 2,640 gallons of rum and other goods, they arrived in Massachusetts, where the child caught the attention of a man named John. He purchased her as a gift for his wife Susannah Wheatley, who was grieving the loss of their seven-year-old daughter. The young African girl would be named Phillis Wheatley and go on to redefine enslavement during Revolutionary Era New England.

Once Susannah recognized that Phillis had promising potential, she began providing her an education alongside the family's two children. Studying English, Latin, and the Bible became the foundation for Phillis' lifetime of recognition as a writer. Her book, *Poems on Various Subjects, Religious and Moral*, was published in 1773, but only after 18 Massachusetts men tested her intelligence and signed a statement confirming that she, a slave, had, in fact, written her own poetry. Phillis Wheatley became the first African American poet to have her work published.

She was legally freed shortly after but remained by the bedside of Susannah until her death. Phillis struggled with her health and finances for the rest of her life, eventually dying at the age of 30 on the same day as her infant child.

She left a significant imprint of the emerging United States when she wrote a poem for George Washington: *Proceed, great chief, with virtue on thy side, Thy ev'ry action let the Goddess guide*. It's generally agreed the former slave and future president met with each other in Cambridge, Massachusetts.

This building was named for Wheatley in 1920 and housed the first "Colored" YWCA in the country that was founded in 1905 by a Black women's literary group called the Book Lover's Club.

Address 901 Rhode Island Avenue NW, Washington, DC 20001, +1 (202) 847-0971, www.pwywca.org | Getting there Metro to Shaw-Howard U (Green and Yellow Line); bus 63, 64 to 11th Street & Rhode Island Avenue NW | Hours Viewable from the outside only | Tip N Street Village serves nearly 2,000 homeless and low-income women each year. Learn about their services and volunteer opportunities (1333 N Street NW, www.nstreetvillage.org).

77 Phoebe Waterman Haas Public Observatory

An astronomy star

While you could spend days exploring the exhibits at the Smithsonian National Air and Space Museum, an exhibit outside the museum pays tribute to a groundbreaking woman in astronomy. The Phoebe Waterman Haas Public Observatory, opened in 2009, and it was renamed in 2013 for Phoebe Haas.

Phoebe was born in North Dakota in 1882 and began her education as a homeschooled student before moving to Michigan to attend high school. She attended Vassar College, the second degree-granting institution of higher learning for women in the United States, where she earned both her Bachelor of Arts and her Master of Arts in mathematics and astronomy in 1906. The only career path available to women in astronomy was to work as a "computer," analyzing data and making calculations. Harvard Observatory spearheaded this process, hiring all-female teams to do computation and paying them as little as half of what the male teams had previously earned.

Phoebe worked as a computer at the Mount Wilson Observatory in California alongside top astronomers, but she was passionate about the science. She wanted to be a professional astronomer and do her own work. She earned her doctorate in astronomy from the University of California (UC) at Berkeley. She made observations at the Lick Observatory there, and she was one of the first women to operate a major telescope. Another female classmate, Anna Estelle Glancy, graduated from UC Berkeley on the same day, but as Haas' dissertation was published first, she is credited as the first US woman to earn a doctorate in astronomy. For many years, Phoebe served as an observer for the American Association of Variable Star Observers, submitting over 300 observations over five years, and financially supporting the organization.

Address Independence Avenue & 4th Street SW, Washington, DC 20560, +1 (202) 633-2517, www.airandspace.si.edu | Getting there Metro to L'Enfant Plaza (Blue, Green, Orange, Silver, and Yellow Line); bus 681, 881 to Independence Avenue & 6th Street SW | Hours See website for hours and events | Tip Be sure to head inside the museum to learn about women in aviation history, such as Willa Brown, the first Black woman to earn a pilot's license in the US (600 Independence Avenue NW, www.airandspace.si.edu).

78_ Puddin'

Toyin Alli serves up divine comfort food

What started out as a pop-up tent at Eastern Market has grown into one of the city's most sought-after purveyors of comfort food. Over the last decade, Puddin' has expanded into Union Market, two mobile food trucks, and a commercial kitchen. The savory, Southern-style entrées on the menu are divine, but you must not miss the Brown Butter Bourbon Bread Puddin'.

Owner Toyin Alli is the master chef behind these dishes, and she's also part storyteller with a pinch of activism. Through her food, she advocates for her ancestors; through her business she advocates for her community. In June of 2020, Alli campaigned for Black-owned businesses to have a seat at the table – that is vendor tables at the Dupont Circle Farmers Market. While she believes there is still work to be done, successfully entering the market gave locals easier access to her traditional Cajun Creole food, which she believes to be "the true American cuisine."

She recognizes the melting pot of cultural influences in New Orleans but has developed a menu that deconstructs dishes down to their most authentic versions. Toyin's recipes are mindfully researched to honor her ancestors. Her gumbo, for instance, skips the French-style roux and includes ingredients that traditionally reflect West African cuisine, like okra, meat, and tomatoes. She uses sassafras just as her enslaved ancestors and Native people would have, attempting to mimic okra that was unavailable to them. She cooks with crawfish, chicken sausage, and smoked meat to create those divine Southern comfort food dishes, like Étouffée, Red Beans N'Rice, and Shrimp N'Grits.

Toyin was inspired by her mom, who taught her the basics of cooking and encouraged her to experiment in the kitchen growing up. Now, Toyin's mother manages the Union Market location and continues to test and create recipes for Puddin' with her daughter.

Address 1309 5th Street NE, Washington, DC 20002, +1 (202) 725-1030, www.dcpuddin.com, info@dcpuddin.com | Getting there Metro to NoMa-Gallaudet (Red Line); bus 90, 92 to Florida Avenue & 5th Street NE | Hours Daily 11am–8pm | Tip Artist Leda Black and The Female Power Project is one of Eastern Market's top vendor for activist swag, including prints, pins, cards, and clothing (225 7th Street SE, www.ledablack.com).

79_ The REACH

Reimagining a historic performing arts venue

The John F. Kennedy Center for the Performing Arts, named in 1964 as a memorial to the assassinated president and opened to the public in 1971, is the city's premier arts venue. Located along the Potomac River, the theatre welcomes two million visitors a year to over 2,000 performances and exhibits. In 2019, it opened its doors further to the community by expanding the campus to honor Kennedy's vision and legacy across new frontiers.

This sprawling expansion, dubbed a "living theatre," is meant to open access between visitor, performer, artist, and audience in an immersive and responsive experience. This idea is particularly embodied in the art installed throughout the REACH. One piece, *The Courage Within Me*, encourages the viewer to move and turn the 60 panels to reveal a kaleidoscope of colors and messages that explore how you define courage and why courage matters.

This artistic endeavor was spearheaded by artist Michelle Angela Ortiz, in collaboration with art teachers and students from Anacostia High School, Columbia Heights Educational Campus, Dunbar High School, and Eastern High School. The students worked with Ortiz and a team of Kennedy Center educational artists to delve into the concept of being courageous and embodying courage every day – and translating their reflections into writings and paintings.

Michelle Angela Ortiz is a visual artist, muralist, and community arts educator, whose art is a vehicle for representing people and communities whose histories are often lost or co-opted. Over the past 20 years, she has designed and created large-scale public works across the country and around the world, often using her art as a bridge to social justice. Her collaboration with the Kennedy Center on this work brings together the voices of the youth generation, the history of this renowned artistic space, and the promise of a brighter future for all.

Address 2700 F Street NW, Washington, DC 20566, +1 (202) 416-8000, www.kennedy-center.org/reach | Getting there Metro to Foggy Bottom-GWU (Blue, Orange, and Silver Line); bus 80 to Virginia Avenue & 25th Street NW | Hours See website for event schedule | Tip Studio Gallery is the longest running artist-owned gallery in DC, founded by artist and DC native Jennie Lea Knight in 1956. Drop by for contemporary art, events, and more (2108 R Street NW, www.studiogallerydc.com).

80 Republic Restoratives
Pia Carusone & Rachel Gardner, founding mothers

A distillery tour of Republic Restoratives goes beyond sampling spirits to deliver the story of a community forward operation in the heart of Ivy City. Tour participants enter the stylish tasting room before traveling upstairs to an event space where the smell of bourbon and the sight of wooden barrels bring a rustic vibe to Washington, DC.

How did this establishment come to be? Imagine an empty warehouse with gravel floors full of nothing more than the vision of co-founders Pia Carusone and Rachel Gardner. After these women bought the building and sketched plans, they set up two beach chairs, some plastic crates, and a camera to record a video campaign calling for the support of investors. Republic Restoratives would surpass their fundraising goal to become the largest crowdfunded distillery in the history of the United States.

It's not uncommon for these founding mothers of the DC distillery scene to make bold moves and brave statements. The brand was built on celebrating disruptive attitudes, exemplified by some of their politically inspired spirit names, like "Rodham Rye" in honor of Hillary Clinton, who was running for president when the distillery opened in 2016. Situated in the nation's capital, Republic Restoratives has stayed true to American values while attempting to "redefine the future of tradition." The logo is designed to show the letter R in American Sign Language, a salute to nearby Gallaudet University (see ch. 39), an institution for students in higher education, who are deaf or hard-of-hearing.

Mindfulness is woven through the distillery's brand and products. Pick up a bottle of Civic Vodka and feel the Republic Restoratives design of a slender bottle that fits more perfectly in feminine hands. That same bottle is stamped with the framework of Washington, a diamond label shaped like the original 100-square-miles border of the nation's early federal city.

Address 1369 New York Avenue NE, Washington, DC 20002, +1 (202) 733-3996, www.republicrestoratives.com | Getting there Bus D4 to Fenwick & Okie Streets NE | Hours See website | Tip Before moving into their house on Kearny Street in Brookland, Lucy Diggs Slowe and Mary Burrill lived in the Ivy City neighborhood (see ch. 89) (1758 T Street NE).

81 Red Door Salon
Elizabeth Arden builds a beauty empire

Is there anything more adorable than travel-sized toiletries? When Elizabeth Arden introduced this innovation to the world, women would be empowered to skip the expensive luggage fees and pack their carry-on bags with those little bottles of feminine beauty. The company was a pioneer in the cosmetics industry, introducing American women to eye makeup and hiring a network of saleswomen to travel, share, and demonstrate products.

The entrepreneur behind this venture was Florence Nightingale Graham, an immigrant, who founded a salon with her business partner Elizabeth Hubbard in New York City. They painted the door red to stand out but when the partnership broke up, Graham adopted the name Elizabeth Arden and would be known by this name until the day she died as the sole owner of Red Door Salon. History remembers Arden as a successful business mogul, but her name suggests the path she took before entering the beauty industry.

As a nurse, Arden worked with various burn lotions that offered medicinal benefits for patients. She used her experience in pharmaceuticals to develop skincare products that would highlight women's natural beauty. She opened her business in 1910, and two years later she marched down 5th Avenue handing out red lipstick to women's suffrage activists. She would go on to create "Montezuma Red," the only lipstick that women Marines were allowed to wear because it matched with their uniforms during World War II. With a shortage of nylon, Elizabeth Arden sold "Velva Leg Film" for women to paint their legs the color of stockings.

In 1929, Arden bought this six-story, Georgian-revival building on Connecticut Avenue in Washington, DC and transformed it into a Red Door Salon. This area was attracting high-end establishments at the time. The building was home to the salon until 1990, and it still stands today with its notable red awnings.

Address 1147 Connecticut Avenue NW, Washington, DC 20036, www.avigailoren.com/
elizabeth-arden-building | Getting there Metro to DuPont Circle (Red Line); bus 42, 43 to
Connecticut Avenue & M Street NW | Hours Unrestricted from outside only | Tip Hanging
in the National Portrait Gallery is a portrait of Polish immigrant Helena Rubenstein,
who became a self-made millionaire in the beauty industry and a rival to Elizabeth Arden
(8th & G Streets NW, www.npg.si.edu).

82 Rosa Parks SafeHouse

Healing and friendship at the Mansion on O Street

When Rosa Louise McCauley Parks refused to give up her seat on a segregated bus, she was a 42-year-old activist in Montgomery, Alabama. But in 1994, at the age of 81, she was attacked and beaten in her Detroit apartment. Too traumatized to stay at home, she found herself in Washington, DC, seeking refuge and healing at the O Street Museum and Mansion.

The museum founder H. H. Leonard accepted Parks into her hotel as part of the Heroes in Residence program. A stay that was only meant to last a few days turned into years, and the mansion became a second home for Rosa Parks, who lived here on and off through the final decade of her life. Leonard developed a beautiful friendship with her beloved guest and earned the nickname "Lady H." She has admitted that she didn't even know who Rosa Parks was when they met in 1994. It would be years later when she finally learned about the contributions and legacy of this equal rights activist. Leonard believes this blind faith and acceptance is why the two friends could communicate so openly and form such an important, genuine, and everlasting bond.

Their time spent together was not without incident, however. During a Sunday Gospel Brunch in honor of Rosa Parks' birthday, the neighbors across the street called the police and claimed that "people of another color" were breaking into the mansion and disturbing the peace. After the situation had been de-escalated, Lady H apologized and received a response from Rosa Parks that would deeply impact the future of the Mansion on O. She said, "Dear, this is okay. When those people go to sell their house, you need to buy it for me. That's how you deal with racism." Lady H did exactly that. She bought the house across the street, and today it stands as the Rosa Parks SafeHouse. Leonard stayed loyal to Parks until the day she died, even serving as a pallbearer at her funeral.

Address 2020 O Street NW, Washington, DC 20036, +1 (202) 496-2070, www.omansion.com | Getting there Metro to DuPont Circle (Red Line); bus G2 to P & 20th Streets NW | Hours Daily 11am–5pm | Tip Before Venus and Serena Williams, Georgetown residents Margaret and Roumania Peter were recognized as top athletes on the Black tennis circuit in the 1940s. The courts in Rose Park where they practiced are named for the sisters (2609 Dumbarton Street NW, www.roseparkdc.org).

83 Rosedale Community Center

Mamie "Peanut" Johnson, a field of her own

Nicknamed "Peanut" because of her petite size, Mamie Johnson defied the odds and stood tall on the dirt mound as the first and only woman to pitch in the Negro Leagues. Two other ballplayers, Toni Stone and Connie Morgan, are recorded as the only other women in the league's history.

Mamie "Peanut" Johnson attended a tryout in Alexandria, VA for the All-American Girls Professional Baseball League but was rejected because of racial segregation. Later that year, she was recruited at 18 years old to the Indianapolis Clowns. She would play three seasons total, finishing her career with a batting average around .270 and a pitching record of 33-8.

Born Mamie Belton, she lived as a teenager in Washington, DC with her mother Della Belton Havelow, who owned a house in the H Street Corridor. Peanut would often play sandlot baseball at the nearby playground that is now Rosedale Community Center. It was here where a scout discovered Johnson for the first time and recruited her to play professional baseball in the Negro Leagues. In April of 2013, this field was dedicated in honor of Mamie "Peanut" Johnson, whose name now stretches across the scoreboard. This is the first athletic field in the District of Columbia that the Department of Parks and Recreation had named for a woman.

Though her legacy runs deep in the sport of baseball, Johnson dedicated most of her adult life to a career in nursing. She would provide nursing care for three decades at local Sibley Memorial Hospital. She also ran a Negro Leagues memorabilia store in Mitchellville, MD. In 2008, Major League Baseball teams drafted living players from the Negro Leagues, and Mamie "Peanut" Johnson would officially become a member of the Washington Nationals.

Address 1701 Gales Street NE, Washington, DC 20002, +1 (202) 727-2591, www.dpr.dc.gov/
page/rosedale-community-center-00, dpr@dc.gov | Getting there Metro to Stadium
Armory (Blue, Orange, and Silver Line); bus X2 to Benning Road & 17th Street NE | Hours
Mon–Fri 10am–9pm, Sat 9am–5pm | Tip Grab an original chili half-smoke from Ben's
Chili Bowl, the iconic U Street restaurants started by Virginia and Ben Ali in 1958. Just outside
is a mural of Mamie "Peanut" Johnson by DC artist Aniekan Udofia (1213 U Street NW,
www.benschilibowl.com).

84__Ruth Bader Ginsburg Mural

A significant gesture by a woman-owned company

In the alleyways of the U Street Corridor is a larger-than-life mural of Ruth Bader Ginsburg, honoring the trailblazer as a champion for equality. Her reputation as the "Notorious RBG" is a cultural phenomenon. Her presence as a petite and soft-spoken Supreme Court Justice is a contrast to her legacy as a social justice giant.

Visitors might easily recognize the standard elements in artist Rose Jaffe's masterpiece, such as the black robe or RBG's iconic dissent collar, but the significance of this mural can't be captured at first glance. Absorbing this art requires a deeper look at those colorful birds flying freely from the justice's hands. They symbolize CEO Lisa Wise, who commissioned this mural in celebration of Flock DC, the parent company of property management brands Nest, Roost, and Starling DC.

The bird theme comes from family history, when Wise's grandmother became an award-winning artist by painting naturalist subjects, mostly birds. Lisa Wise was also inspired by her mother, a ceramicist and printmaker, whom she describes as nothing short of a second wave feminist during the 1970s, a "newly-minted divorcee," who campaigned for progressive values at the same time Ginsburg was rising in the ranks of the ACLU. The Ginsburg mural was commissioned by a family of fierce women, who understood the power of art and activism. It's an example of how the passion of one generation becomes embedded in the soul and work of the next.

Reflecting on the dedication ceremony in September 2018, CEO Lisa Wise shared these words, "As I joined so many others at the mural to honor Justice Ginsburg this weekend, I did so promising her – and my mom, and my grandmother – to fight for a just tomorrow. I have them to thank for reminding me that breaking those barriers isn't just my right as a woman; indeed, it's my obligation."

Address 1508 U Street NW, Washington, DC 20009, +1 (202) 540-8038, www.flock-dc.com, hello@flock-dc.com | Getting there Metro to U Street (Green and Yellow Line); bus 52, 54 to 14th & U Streets NW | Hours Unrestricted | Tip Lady Clipper Barber Shop is a woman-owned salon where entrepreneur Lesley Bryant, a graduate of Corcoran College of Art and Design, showcases the work of local artists on the walls of her shop (1514 U Street NW, www.theladyclipper.com).

85 Sakakawea Statue

A courageous young woman led the way

Native peoples from the Mandan, Hidatsa, and Arikara Nation gathered at the Washington Monument for a horseback parade in 2013. Chairman Tex Hall led the procession to the United States Capitol Building, where the tribe erected teepees and danced. Later that day, Hall helped unveil the statue of Sakakawea in the Capitol Rotunda, honoring her for her service to the country as a traveler, guide, translator, diplomat, wife, and mother. *Sakakawea*, meaning "Bird Woman," was sculpted by artist Leonard Crunelle, whose model for the sculpture was Mink Woman, Sakakawea's granddaughter.

Sakakawea's tragic story began at the age of 12, when she was trafficked from her Shoshone tribe in what's now North Dakota, and forced into marriage with her captor, a 46-year-old polygamist named Toussaint Charbonneau. Written records indicate that he was a violent domestic abuser, harming Sakakawea and other girls. Nevertheless, she accompanied him and 32 other men known as "the Corps" on the Lewis and Clark expedition (1803–1806). She was qualified to serve as a translator, guide, and plant gatherer, but her presence was of particular interest to the Corp because as a woman, she was a symbol of peace to the other Native people they might encounter.

Sakakawea became pregnant while on the expedition at age 16. She was induced into labor using rattlesnake rattles and gave birth on a freezing day in February. Her son was nicknamed "Pomp," meaning "First Child" in Shoshone, and she courageously carried him on her back throughout the journey.

Sakakawea is represented in more statues than any other American woman. The statue in the Capitol Rotunda was funded by the General Federation of Women's Clubs of North Dakota and is a replica of one in the State Capitol. Her image is also on the gold $1 coin designed by Glenna Goodacre, sculptor of the Vietnam Women's Memorial (see ch. 100).

Address First Street SE, Washington, DC 20004, www.aoc.gov/explore-capitol-campus/art/sakakawea | **Getting there** Metro to Capitol South (Blue, Orange, and Silver Line); bus 30N, 30S, 32, 36 to Independence & New Jersey Avenues SE | **Hours** See website | **Tip** The General Federation of Women's Clubs was founded by journalist Jane Cunningham Croly after she was barred from an all-male press club dinner. The headquarters is a National Historic Landmark (1734 N Street, NW, www.gfwc.org).

NORTH DAKOTA

SAKAKAWEA
A MEMBER OF THE
LEWIS AND CLARK EXPEDITION

1804 – 1806

86   Sara Andrews Spencer Grave

A resting place for a women's rights fighter

Among the elaborate Victorian and Art Nouveau monuments in Glenwood Cemetery, a historic burial ground founded in 1852, you will spot more than one obelisk. Look for the tall gray structure honoring Sara Andrews Spencer, a pioneer who dedicated her life to advancing the cause of equality for women.

Born in 1837 in New York, Sara grew up disillusioned with a society where women were treated as less than equal. In 1871, she joined with 72 other women in DC in an effort to register and vote, an illegal action at that time. When the women were refused, they brought a lawsuit before the Supreme Court of the District of Columbia. The judge ruled that women were citizens but required local legislation to vote. The Supreme Court would uphold this decision in 1874.

In 1876, Sara joined Susan B. Anthony at a centennial celebration in Philadelphia, where the women staged a protest of being denied a place in the program. They crashed the stage to present the Declaration of Rights of the Women of the United States. Pandemonium ensued as the women distributed copies to the men gathered.

Sara dedicated her life to the cause of suffrage, actively serving in the National Woman Suffrage Association and presiding over the Woman Franchise Association of the District of Columbia. She traveled around the country in support of women's rights and became the first woman to address a committee at the Republican National Convention, when she spoke in support of women's suffrage in 1876.

Sara's dedication to the cause was legendary. An editorial in *The Woman's Exponent* described her as "the woman who is behind the curtain doing the work of a dozen women, all for the benefit of her sex." Unfortunately, she died in 1909, 10 years before Congress would pass the 19th Amendment.

Address 2219 Lincoln Road NE, Washington, DC 20002, +1 (202) 667-1016,
www.theglenwoodcemetery.com | Getting there Bus D8 to Franklin Street NE &
Glenwood Cemetery | Hours Daily 6am–8pm | Tip The Brookland neighborhood is
also home to Bluebird Sky Yoga, where owner Jennie Light creates a welcoming space
for yogis at every level. Light is a former radio show host, so music is a key component
to classes here (3101 12th Street NE, www.bluebirdskyyoga.com).

87 _ Saturday Night Salons

Georgia Douglas Johnson's cultural renaissance

Every Saturday night for nearly two decades, Georgia Douglas Johnson opened her house to the city's most prominent writers, artists, and leaders in the Black community. These attendees were known as "Saturday Nighters," and they gathered for weekly salons at Johnson's home in the U Street Corridor, marked with a plaque.

Her salon events were opportunities to exchange ideas and participate in intellectual conversations. Johnson referred to her residence on S Street as "a halfway house" because her vision was for people with diverse opinions to communicate openly in this space with the intent of meeting "half-way" in the middle. From political debates to sharing original works of art, the "S Street Salons" earned a reputation for being one of the city's most cultured events.

The 1920s and 1930s were a cultural renaissance for artists. Northern cities like Washington, DC were incubators for the New Negro Movement in this era of rising Black pride, expression, and consciousness. Johnson supported and unified this emerging community of thought leaders, including Alice Dunbar Nelson, Zora Neale Hurston, Carter G. Woodson and Angelina Weld Grimké, some of whom were likely involved in the gay community as well.

Johnson was a DC schoolteacher and worked for the Department of Labor, but she would ultimately become known as one of the most widely read poets of her time. As a widow and woman of color, her poems reflected the intersection of her gender and her diverse racial background as the daughter of Native American, African American and English parents. She wrote a syndicated newspaper column and led the Washington Social Letter Club. It's quite agreed upon that Georgia Douglas Johnson was an accomplished woman, but it has been said that she would also write under the alias of "Mary Strong" so historians may never know the full extent of her collection and reach.

Address 1461 S Street NW, Washington, DC 20009, www.dcwritershomes.wdchumanities.
org/georgia-douglas-johnson | Getting there Metro to U Street (Green and Yellow Line);
bus 64 to 11th & S Street NW | Hours View from outside only | Tip Walk by the historic
home of May Miller just two blocks away, another writer and salon hostess (1632 S Street
NW, www.dcwritershomes.wdchumanities.org/may-miller).

88 _Sheep by the Sea_
Wilhelmina Cole Holladay created the NMWA

Hanging on a bright pink wall in the National Museum of Women in the Arts (NMWA) is a painting titled _Sheep by the Sea_ by artist Rosa Bonheur. Bonheur's 1865 work, part of the Museum Founder's Collection, represents every woman in this museum: talented artists denied recognition. Before Wilhelmina Cole Holladay created this space, it would have been extremely unlikely to find a major art museum that focuses exclusively on women. NMWA was the first in the world and remains a distinct champion for women in the arts.

Holladay's personal story sets the foundation for this journey toward representation. As a child, she was influenced by her grandmother, who had a Rosa Bonheur print hanging in her library. Holladay studied art history in Paris, served at the Pentagon during World War II, and worked at the Chinese Embassy for Madame Chiang Kai-shek. Her art career started at the National Gallery of Art (see ch. 69) as a tour guide and gift shop assistant. Her first purchase was a $100 painting from the Arlington High School art fair, and her second a $200 Renoir print.

As her knowledge of art grew, she started questioning the lack of representation and would playfully challenge guests at dinner parties to name five women artists. She even began offering art tours inside her Georgetown home. Holladay's collection turned into a potential museum when she consulted with her friend Nancy Hanks (see ch. 75), the second person to chair the National Endowment for the Arts. The National Museum of Women in the Arts opened its doors in 1987, and it remains the legacy of Holladay, who passed in 2021.

NMWA closed its building for long-term renovations in 2021, but the museum's ongoing range of programming allows visitors to continue engaging through virtual events, by exploring public art installations around the city streets. The museum's shop that features items made by women will also be open online.

Address 1250 New York Avenue NW, Washington, DC 20005, +1 (202) 783-5000, www.nmwa.org | Getting there Metro to Metro Center (Red, Orange, Silver, and Blue Line); bus X2, 80, G8, X9 to H & 13th Streets NW | Hours Mon–Sat 10am–5pm, Sun noon–5pm | Tip The Hirshhorn Museum strives to bring art to new spaces within its building. Look for Barbara Kruger's *Belief+Doubt*, which wraps the entire lower-level museum space – walls, floors, escalators – in text-printed vinyl (Independence Avenue & 7th Street, www.hirshhorn.si.edu).

89 Slowe-Burrill House
The secret herstory of a Brookland home

Lucy Diggs Slowe and Mary Burrill were two Black women in a committed lesbian relationship... most likely. These successful and highly respected educators moved into this house together in 1922, at a time when sociopolitical norms would have bullied the queer community into remaining discreet. Living in the margins, Lucy and Mary would lead very different lives in public than in private.

While society might have accepted these women as roommates, Slowe and Burrill would embrace their same-sex relationship in the company of trusted friends. It was common for them to welcome visitors like Georgia Douglas Johnson (see ch. 87) or students from Howard University, where Slowe served as the first Dean of Women. She graduated as valedictorian in 1908 and would leave a legacy as one of the original nine founders of Alpha Kappa Alpha sorority (see ch. 1). Today, there is a dorm and a window named in her honor on Howard's campus. Mary Burrill was also quite a remarkable woman, who created progressive art and music. A piece she wrote in 1919 was published in Margaret Sanger's *Birth Control Review*.

Burrill and Slowe built private, homosocial networks made up of predominantly Black female social reformers like themselves. These safe spaces were proven necessary each time they encountered discriminating circumstances in their public lives. One example was when Howard University President J. Stanley Durkee insisted that Slowe move her residence on campus to supervise female student life. She called out his sexism, as male employees were not demanded to do the same in their personal lives.

Lucy Slowe would remain in her house on Kearny Street with her beloved Mary Burrill until Slowe died in 1937. Complicated paperwork would cause Burrill to move out of the only house Slowe had ever owned. She moved into an apartment, where she was known to keep white carnations on her piano, next to a photo of Lucy.

Address 1256 Kearny Street NE, Washington, DC 20017, https://historicsites.
dcpreservation.org/items/show/1085 | Getting there Metro to Brookland-CUA (Red Line);
bus H8 to 12th & Kearny Streets NE | Hours Viewable from the outside only | Tip Mary
Burrill directed the Washington Conservatory of Music and School of Expression alongside
the founder Harriett Gibbs-Marshall (902 T Street NW, www.culturaltourismdc.org).

90 The Spirit of Nursing
Memorializing Jane Delano, nursing revolutionary

Among the neoclassical buildings at the American Red Cross Headquarters stands a shrouded bronze figure. A cape covers her head, and her arms are outstretched. This mysterious figure is the sculpture *Spirit of Nursing*, a memorial to nursing pioneer Jane A. Delano and to the 296 nurses who lost their lives in World War I.

Delano began her nursing career at a Florida hospital, treating victims of the yellow fever epidemic. From the beginning, Delano developed innovative nursing procedures that increased patient recovery and survival. During the Spanish-American War (1898), Delano joined the New York chapter of the American Red Cross, founded by Clara Barton in 1881 (see ch. 66). Delano continued training and educating nurses at teaching hospitals until 1909, when she was named superintendent of the United States Army Nurse Corps.

While Delano held that post, multiple nursing organizations existed, all with disparate methods and techniques. Delano worked with other leaders in the field to create the Red Cross Nursing Service by uniting the efforts of the American Nurses Association, the Army Nurse Corps, and the American Red Cross. This collaboration yielded a reserve of thousands of registered nurses organized and ready for disaster relief or wartime service.

Delano revolutionized the profession, more than doubling the number of trained nurses for military service, and she provided training, textbooks, and courses for nurses as well. Under her leadership, over 20,000 nurses served bravely during World War I. She died while on a Red Cross mission to France in 1919 and was laid to rest in the Nurse's Section (Section 21) at Arlington National Cemetery. She was awarded the Distinguished Service Medal posthumously. Even in her final moments, her dedication to her profession was unwavering as she spoke her last words, "What about my work, I must get back to my work."

Address 430 17th Street NW, Washington, DC 20006, +1 (800) 733-2767, www.culturaltourismdc.org/portal/american-red-cross | Getting there Metro to Farragut West (Blue, Orange, Red, and Silver Line); bus 7Y, 80 to 18th & E Streets NW | Hours Unrestricted | Tip Email tours@redcross.org to schedule a tour of the Red Cross Head-quarters, designated a National Landmark in 1965. Look for the portrait of Clara Barton, founder of the American Red Cross, painted by Charles Stevenson, who dedicated the piece to his mother (430 17th Street NW, www.redcross.org).

91 — The Star-Spangled Banner

Mary Pickersgill's handiwork is American history

The National Museum of American History is one of the most popular destinations in DC. Visitors from around the world go there to see our national treasures, including our most important flag, the Star-Spangled Banner, which inspired Francis Scott Key to pen the poem that would become our national anthem.

Before the lawyer and poet set pen to paper, a woman named Mary Pickersgill worked diligently to complete two flags for Fort McHenry in Maryland. Mary's mother ran a flag shop and taught her daughter the art of making flags. Mary would marry in 1795 at the age of 19, bear four children, only one of whom would live to adulthood, and find herself a widow by age 29. She was living in Baltimore with her mother and daughter when she received a commission that would change American history.

While the US was fighting Great Britain in the War of 1812, Major George Armistead felt that Fort McHenry was well-prepared for battle but lacked an impressive flag. Armistead led the group that arrived at Mary Pickersgill's shop in 1813 to commission a flag. It was too large for one person to make, so Mary recruited help from her own household and neighbors. She was able to complete the task in six weeks, although she had to move to a local brewery to finish the project, as the flag was too big to fit in her own shop. The finished flag contained 400 yards of fabric, weighed 50 pounds, and included 15 stars and 15 stripes, one for each of the 15 states in the Union. The final flag was delivered to Fort McHenry in August 1813, just before the Battle of Baltimore.

Pickersgill was paid over $400 dollars ($6,700 in today's currency) for her efforts, and her business would boom. She became successful enough to advocate for social issues, such as housing, jobs, and financial assistance for disadvantaged women. She died in 1857 and is buried in Loudon Park Cemetery in Baltimore.

Address 1300 Constitution Avenue NW, Washington, DC 20560, +1 (202) 633-1000, www.americanhistory.si.edu, info@si.edu | Getting there Metro to Smithsonian (Blue, Orange, and Silver Line); bus 697 to Constitution Avenue & 12th Street NW | Hours See website | Tip Across the street at the National Museum of Natural History, keep your eye out for women's contributions to the STEM fields while enjoying fossils, gems, and a walk through the butterfly pavilion (10th Street & Constitution Avenue NW, www.naturalhistory.si.edu).

92 _Students Aspire_ Sculpture
Truth and justice at Howard University

Howard University is a historically Black institution with a significant influence on the society and culture of DC. Established in 1867, the campus is rich with the history of the students who came before in their pursuit of _Veritas et Utilitas_ – Truth and Service.

One of those students was Elizabeth Catlett. Born in DC in 1915, Catlett's grandmother would share stories of her own enslavement. Catlett attended Howard University, though it was not her first choice. She was admitted to Carnegie Institute of Technology but was refused admission when they discovered her race. At Howard, she would study art, but knowing a career as an artist was unusual for a woman of her era, she became a teacher. She would be compelled to fight for equal pay – unsuccessfully.

Her interest in artist Grant Wood inspired her to study at the University of Iowa, where he taught. He encouraged her to create art based on her experiences, so she started depicting the stories of Black women. She would become the first Black woman to graduate from that university with a Master of Fine Arts. Catlett traveled to Mexico, joining the _Taller de Gráfica Popular_, a workshop promoting progressive causes. She was part of this group for 20 years. Due to her activism, she was deemed an "undesirable alien" by the United States Government. In 1962, she renounced her US citizenship and became a citizen of Mexico.

In 1974, just a few years after hosting a solo exhibition at Howard, Catlett was selected to create a sculpture for the School of Engineering building on campus. _Students Aspire_ is a 1.5-ton sculpture featuring a male and female figure with their arms outstretched, supporting each other as they hold a medallion with the equality sign, surrounded by additional medallions celebrating science. The work emphasizes equality – as a scientific concept but also a social one, among genders, races, and backgrounds.

Address 2400 6th Street NW, Washington, DC 20059, +1 (202) 806-6100, www.howard.edu |
Getting there Metro to Shaw-Howard University (Green and Yellow Line); bus 70 to Georgia
Avenue & Barry Place NW | Hours See website for tour information | Tip Howard University
is the alma mater of our first female Vice President, Kamala Harris(see ch. 1). Stroll down
Massachusetts Avenue past the US Naval Observatory to glimpse the Veep's residence and
check the time on the USNO Master Clock (1 Observatory Circle NW, www.usno.navy.mil).

93 Surratt Boarding House

Once the home of a convicted conspirator

At first glimpse, Wok and Roll is just one of several restaurants in DC's bustling Chinatown neighborhood. But behind the neon lights, the historic façade of this restaurant hides a sinister secret.

The building that houses Wok and Roll was once the home of Mary Surratt, the first woman executed by the United States Government. Mary, a native of Maryland and a staunch Catholic, married John Surratt in 1840. She mothered three children while John purchased land in Maryland for a tavern and inn, as well as a townhouse on H Street NW, which they used as a rental property.

As the Civil War began in 1861, the Surratts were openly supportive of the Confederate cause, frequently hosting Confederate supporters and spies. John Surratt passed away suddenly in 1862, leaving Mary in financial crisis. She moved into her DC townhouse full-time, using it as a boarding house for income. She leased her tavern in Maryland to a known Confederate sympathizer. Her son, also named John, was a courier for the Confederate Secret Service, moving messages and money across enemy lines. His work brought various men to the boarding house, including John Wilkes Booth, who grew close to the Surratts.

Mary Surratt would later be accused of keeping "the nest that hatched the egg," the egg being the conspiracy to assassinate Abraham Lincoln (see ch. 34). Members of the conspiracy met in the boarding house repeatedly and hid supplies at the Surratt tavern. Mary was arrested just three days after Lincoln's assassination due to the suspicious company she kept.

Mary Surratt faced a military tribunal, charged with aiding, abetting, concealing, counseling, and harboring the men who were charged with killing Abraham Lincoln and plotting against the Union Government. She was ultimately found guilty and executed on July 7, 1865. It's a story you'll be pondering over your egg rolls and sesame noodles.

Address 604 H Street NW, Washington, DC 20001, +1 (202) 347-4656, www.wokandrolldc.com | Getting there Metro to Gallery Place-Chinatown (Green, Red, and Yellow Line); bus 80, P6, X2, X9 to H & 7th Streets NW | Hours Daily 11am–10pm | Tip See the bed where Abraham Lincoln died in the home of Anna and William Petersen, just across the street from Ford's Theatre (516 10th Street NW, www.nps.gov/foth/the-petersen-house.htm).

94 The Tabard Inn

Matriarchs, movements, and military officers

Three years after her husband drowned at sea, Marie Willoughby Rogers bought the Lippitt Mansion and established the Tabard Inn. She attracted new clients during the prohibition era not by bootlegging gin or rye, but rather by serving a more sophisticated drink: tea.

Restaurant culture in the early 1900s was predominantly masculine, prioritizing large meals and often requiring that women have a male chaperone. In the decade following suffrage, recently liberated women were not only exercising their right to vote, but they were also empowered to build independent spaces of their own. Marie Rogers and other women became entrepreneurs by opening tea houses that catered to femininity. The American Tea Room Movement gained momentum during the Roaring Twenties by offering casual home-cooked meals in a cozy living room setting.

The Tabard Inn became a gathering spot for groups such as the Daughters of the American Revolution (see ch. 35), of which Mrs. Rogers was a member. For three years during World War II, the hotel housed at least 70 women Navy officers known as WAVES and Mrs. Rogers would lead them on guided tours around the Dupont neighborhood. Ownership changed in the 1970s, when local power couple Fritzi Cohen and her husband Edward purchased the business and preserved the buildings. The Tabard Inn remains steeped in women's history with Fritzi at the head. Her love of theater and passion for politics make her a vibrant and edgy force in DC. She said, "Legally, I am the president of the company. And I don't like that word, so I prefer to call myself 'Matriarch.'" The Cohens structured the business to be 51 percent majority-owned by employees. Visitors today will surely be charmed by the staff's warm hospitality and the inn's quaint old English decor. The Tabard is a perfect spot for a cozy weekend brunch or an intimate dinner – be sure to try the oxtail!

Address 1739 N Street NW, Washington, DC 20036, +1 (202) 931-5137, www.tabardinn.com | Getting there Metro to Dupont Circle (Red Line); bus 42, 43, to Connecticut Avenue & N Street NW | Hours See website for restaurant hours | Tip After a career in government, Danielle Vogel founded Glen's Garden Market to fight climate change and prioritize the environment through sourcing sustainably, minimizing food waste, and supporting small local producers (2001 S Street NW, www.glensgardenmarket.com).

95 Teaism

Michelle, Linda, and Lela share the integrity of tea

Lela Singh was just a young girl in 1996 when her mother Michelle Brown founded Teaism with her business partner Linda Nuemann. She would spend her childhood watching the two women run a business with passion and purpose. As a working mother, Michelle gave Lela responsibilities, like wiping down tables in the café, ultimately teaching her a strong work ethic while introducing her to the family business. Linda took on an aunt-like role and would look after Lela at work and in the family apartment above Teaism Penn Quarter.

After working in the non-profit sector out of college, Lela returned to Teaism and would play a pivotal role in the operations. She took lead on significant projects, like managing social media, replying to correspondence, and unofficially being a tiebreaker in some decisions the two founders might disagree on.

The matriarchal culture of Teaism is just one contributing element to their success, but it needs to be stated boldly that Michelle and Linda are pioneers in the service industry. They adopted business practices that were wildly advanced in the 1990s but have since trickled into the mainstream. Teaism introduced their clientele to the unexplored culture of tea paired with responsibly sourced food into a fast casual environment.

Michelle and Linda took a drink that Americans commonly thought of as "medicine in a bag with a string" and exposed the natural integrity and diversity of loose-leaf tea. They infused healthy, Asian-inspired food into DC's food scene. Teaism defined what it meant to be a fast casual café during an era of fine dining. They were mindful of avoiding food waste and implementing sustainable practices years before the world caught up.

It's not uncommon to see tables reserved for a book talk or birthday luncheon at their café. Teaism is a neighborhood gathering place with global appeal, where creativity is steeped with tradition.

Address 2009 R Street NW, Washington, DC 20009, +1 (202) 667-3827, www.teaism.com |
Getting there Metro to Dupont Circle (Red Line); bus S9 to 16th & U Streets NW | Hours
Daily 11am–8pm | Tip Visit the FRESHFARM DuPont Circle Market on Sunday mornings
to shop for local produce (1600 20th Street NW, www.freshfarm.org/markets/dupont-circle).

96 The Temperance Fountain

A maligned monument to a misunderstood movement

In the midst of downtown DC stands one of the last remnants of the once-powerful temperance movement. The Temperance Fountain, installed in 1884 at the bequest of Dr. Henry Cogswell, who designed fountains in several cities, was meant to provide DC residents with free, clean drinking water as an alternative to alcohol. Cogswell's experiment was short-lived, as maintenance was costly, and the fountains weren't very popular. Over time, most of the fountains across the country were removed or destroyed.

The *Washington Post* called the fountain "the city's ugliest statue," but the fountain stands as a testament to a movement largely guided by and for women. The American temperance movement began building steam in the 1820s, spurred by organizations led primarily by women, such as the Women's Christian Temperance Union (WCTU) and the Anti-Saloon League. It is not surprising that women were drawn to this cause. It gave women rare political agency, and women were directly impacted by the excesses of alcohol consumption. In the 1890s, Americans drank three times as much as they drank in the 2010s, and domestic violence rates skyrocketed. For many women, this movement was a lifeline to a better quality of life and safety in their own homes.

There was a great deal of overlap between the temperance movement and other social movements involving women in the 19th century, including abolition and suffrage. Many suffrage leaders in the 1800s, including Susan B. Anthony, saw giving women the vote as the first step to gaining prohibition of alcohol via the ballot box. Frances Willard, National President of the WCTU, spent 10 years spearheading the organization's temperance efforts, while also advocating for women's suffrage. Willard believed both movements shared the goal of giving women an active role in improving society. She stated, "Politics is the place for women."

Address 678 Indiana Avenue NW, Washington, DC 20004, https://historicsites.
dcpreservation.org | Getting there Metro to Archives-Navy Memorial-Penn Quarter
(Green and Yellow Line); bus 70, 74, 79 to Pennsylvania Avenue & 7th Street NW |
Hours Unrestricted | Tip Up the street is HipCityVeg, founded by Nicole Marquis.
The fast-casual vegan restaurant strives to make plant-based food accessible, affordable,
and delicious (712 7th Street NW, www.hipcityveg.com).

97__Terrell Place

Mary Church Terrell, lifting as she climbed

At the corner of 7th and F Streets NW, once the site of Hecht's department store, stands a complex named for Mary Church Terrell. Hecht's, founded in Baltimore in 1857, embodied the modern shopping experience. Their stores in downtown DC boasted the first parking garage and elevator. The city's oldest department store chain, Hecht's would offer integrated but unequal shopping for Black customers, who were not permitted in the store's cafeteria.

The segregated lunch counter led to action by the Coordinating Committee for the Enforcement of DC Anti-Discrimination Laws (CCEAD). The organization was founded in 1950 by civil rights activists, including Mary Church Terrell. At age 87, Terrell was chosen to chair the group and actively organized pickets at the store in 1951. By January 1952, Hecht's announced that they would integrate all areas of the store.

Born in Tennessee during the Civil War, Terrell attended Oberlin College as one of the first Black women to enroll and ultimately became one of the first two Black women to earn a Master of Arts, alongside Anna Julia Cooper (see ch. 8). She was an educator at Dunbar High School, co-founded the Colored Women's League, and served as the first president of the National Association of Colored Women (NACW). She went on to create the National Association of College Women, and she became the first Black woman in the country to serve on a city's Board of Education.

As a journalist, she advocated for civil rights, suffragism, and other progressive issues. In 1949, after being refused service at the popular Thompson's Restaurant, Terrell organized a lawsuit, which led to a legal battle and a Supreme Court decision overturning segregation laws in DC. The bronze plaque at the intersection of 7th and F Streets, on the corner of the building, is a small reminder of Terrell's immense impact on the city.

Address 575 7th Street NW, Washington, DC 20004, www.terrellplace.com | Getting there
Metro to Gallery Place-Chinatown (Green, Red, and Yellow Line); bus 70, 74 to 7th &
E Streets NW | Hours Unrestricted | Tip Head to LeDroit Park to see Mary Church Terrell's
home. Now privately owned, it was designated a National Historic Landmark in 1975
(326 T Street NW, www.nps.gov/places/washington-dc-mary-church-terrell-house.htm).

98_ The *Titanic* Memorial

Gertrude Vanderbilt Whitney's haunting tribute

The sinking of the RMS *Titanic* in 1912 is one of history's greatest tragedies. The ship, lauded as unsinkable, struck an iceberg on April 14th and would be completely submerged shortly after 2am on April 15th, taking with it the lives of more than 1,500 people on board.

The Women's Titanic Memorial Association was created to collect funds to build a memorial in DC honoring the men who sacrificed themselves to save women and children on board. More than 25,000 women across the country made donations.

In 1914, a design contest – open only to women – was held to find an artist to create the memorial. Gertrude Vanderbilt Whitney was selected as the winner. Whitney was one of the wealthiest women in America and a passionate sculptor, art collector, and patron of women in the arts (see ch. 35). Early in her career, she worked under a fake name so that her work could be judged on its own merit. By 1910, she was exhibiting her work with her actual name attached and winning competitions, holding her first solo show in New York City in 1916. After the Metropolitan Museum of Art refused her donation of nearly 700 works of art, she created her own modern art museum, which evolved into the Whitney Museum of American Art.

Her design for the *Titanic* Memorial reflected her signature style. It is an abstract statue of a partially clad man, his arms outstretched in a protective pose. It's carved from one piece of red granite and stands 13 feet tall. While the sculpture was completed in 1920, it stood in a private gallery in New York City before finally being erected on site in 1930. The dedication ceremony took place on May 26, 1931. Helen Taft, who was First Lady when the *Titanic* sank and made the first contribution towards the creation of the memorial, unveiled the statue. It was originally located near Rock Creek Parkway but was relocated to its current spot in 1968 due to construction of the John F. Kennedy Center for the Performing Arts.

Address Southwest Waterfront Park, Washington, DC 20005, www.nps.gov/places/000/
titanic-memorial.htm | Getting there Metro to Waterfront (Green Line); bus 74 to
P & 4th Streets SW | Hours Unrestricted | Tip At nearby Arena Stage, Artistic Director
Molly Smith oversees the largest theater company in the country dedicated to American
plays and playwrights (1101 6th Street SW, www.arenastage.org).

99 Tudor Place

Washington women preserve America's story

Nestled over five and a half acres, Tudor Place is home to over 200 years of American history. The land was purchased in 1805 by Martha Parke Custis Peter, known as Patty, and her husband Thomas. Patty was the granddaughter of Martha Washington and step-granddaughter of George Washington. She was born at Mount Vernon and spent time there growing up. When George Washington died, Patty received an inheritance that enabled her to purchase Tudor Place.

Patty hired William Thornton, architect of the Capitol, to design the mansion as a family home for their children, including three daughters named Columbia, America, and Britannia. Britannia was born at Tudor Place in 1815 and would recall a visit from the Marquis de Lafayette as a child. She was educated at Georgetown's Visitation Convent and was a regular on the society scene, meeting Commodore Beverley Kennon at a party at Octagon House (see ch. 71). She married him at Tudor Place in 1842, but tragically, Kennon died in an explosion, leaving Britannia alone with their four-year-old daughter.

Her mother's death in 1854 made Britannia the matron of the Tudor Place estate, and she would hold that distinction longer than any other owner. She would see the property through the Civil War, when she opened it as a boarding house and refused to house General Grant's wife. And she guarded the family's treasures, many of which came directly from George and Martha Washington. Britannia was involved with a wide array of philanthropic and civic groups, including the Society of Colonial Dames and the Daughters of the American Revolution (see ch. 35).

Britannia died at Tudor Place in 1911 at the age of 95, one day shy of her 96th birthday, and was buried at nearby Oak Hill Cemetery (see ch. 40). Her grandson Armistead Peter would become the sole owner of the property, and her great grandson Armistead Peter III set up a foundation to allow the home and gardens to be open to the public.

Address 1644 31st Street NW, Washington, DC 20007, +1 (202) 965-0400, www.tudorplace.org, info@tudorplace.org | Getting there Bus D2, D6 to Q & 31st Streets NW | Hours See website | Tip Georgetown is home to Take Care, a holistic spa and retailer of natural skincare and beauty products. Founder Becky Waddell's first brick and mortar store is a soothing and engaging space, designed to foster community and host events (1338 Wisconsin Avenue NW, www.takecareshopdc.com).

100 Vietnam Women's Memorial

Welcome home, daughters of America

Army Nurse Diane Carlson Evans returned from Vietnam only to begin fighting a new battle over gender equality for the nearly 265,000 military and civilian women who had served. She was present at the dedication of the Vietnam Veteran's Memorial in 1982. But when *Three Soldiers*, a statue of three men, was added to the memorial in 1984, women who had served as nurses and in other significant roles realized their place in American history had been overlooked once again.

Carlson Evans led a decade-long campaign to establish the Vietnam Women's Memorial, insisting that women take their rightful spot on the National Mall. The committees that approved *Three Soldiers* were quick to reject a statue honoring women. Carlson recalls one of the most outrageous excuses that building a memorial for women would create an obligation to erect a memorial for the canine unit as well.

The project was not without male support. There are numerous accounts of male veterans who were proud to be memorialized alongside the women who cared for them and, in many cases, saved their lives. Carlson admits that she focused primarily on the role of nurses early in the project, but the contributions of civilian women who served and sacrificed were also considered in the design by artist Glenna Goodacre, who sculpted four figures – three women and one wounded man – without any military insignia on their uniforms as an abstract representation of all who contributed.

The Vietnam Women's Memorial was dedicated on November 11, 1993 during a ceremony entitled "A Celebration of Patriotism and Courage." Diane Carlson Evans saw her vision become a reality on that day and declared, "We are dedicating a beautiful monument that portrays all that is good about women's service, all that is tragic and horrible about war, and an everlasting statue that begs for peace."

Address 5 Henry Bacon Drive SW, Washington, DC 20007, +1(877) 463-3647,
www.vietnamwomensmemorial.org, vietnamwomensmemorial@easternnational.org |
Getting there Metro to Foggy Bottom-GWU (Blue, Orange, and Silver Line); bus 7y, H1, L1;
or DC Circulator to Constitution Avenue & 21st Street N | Hours Unrestricted | Tip Find
the names of only eight women on the Vietnam War Memorial: Sharon Lane 23W 112,
Pamela Donovan 53W 43, Annie Graham 48W 12, Mary Klinker 01W 122,
Carol Drazba 05E 47, Eleanor Alexander 31E 08, and Hedwig Orlowski 31E 015.

101 Vladka Meed's Story

A Holocaust story of courage and resistance

How did a woman named Feigele Peltel become Vladka Meed while using an identification card with the name of Stanislawa Wachalska? This is just one of the millions of stories of identity, culture, and resistance told every day at the United States Holocaust Memorial Museum. Opened in 1993, the museum inspires visitors to confront hatred and prevent genocide through its powerful exhibitions and programs of Holocaust history. Much of that history has been gathered from first-person accounts of people's experiences, like that of survivor and educator Feigele Peltel.

Feigele was a member of the Jewish resistance in the Warsaw ghetto from its first days. Born in Warsaw in 1921, she was still a teenager when the Germans invaded Poland. Because she spoke fluent Polish and was assigned outside of the ghetto, she was the perfect candidate to become an underground courier. She took the name Vladka and used her Aryan looks to hide in plain sight. She worked to smuggle weapons across the wall for the Jewish fighters and assisted in smuggling children from the ghetto to hide in Christian homes. She also ran messages among those working in labor camps, those in hiding in the city, and those surviving in the forest. Vladka frequently used fake identification cards and false personas to move easily around Warsaw. She would ultimately participate in the Warsaw Uprising in August 1944 and evacuate out of Poland shortly after.

Vladka, like many survivors, would lose her father to pneumonia in the Warsaw ghetto and her mother, sister, and younger brother to the concentration camp Treblinka. She arrived in New York City on the second ship of survivors from Europe after World War II, along with her husband Benjamin, whom she recruited to the resistance and then fell in love with. She spent the rest of her life tirelessly sharing her story as she worked actively to promote Holocaust education and memorialization.

Address 100 Raoul Wallenberg Place SW, Washington, DC 20010, +1 (202) 488-0400, www.ushmm.org | Getting there Metro to Smithsonian (Blue, Orange, and Silver Line); bus 16E to 52, 54, 59 to 14th & C Streets SW | Hours See website | Tip Sixth & I Historic Synagogue is a center for arts, entertainment, and ideas, while reimaging how religion and community can enhance people's lives. Drop by for one of their popular Jewish Life events or attend a book talk (600 I Street NW, www.sixthandi.org).

THE THINGS I SAW BEGGAR DESCRIPTION . . .
THE VISUAL EVIDENCE AND THE VERBAL
TESTIMONY OF STARVATION, CRUELTY AND
BESTIALITY WERE SO OVERPOWERING . . .
I MADE THE VISIT DELIBERATELY, IN ORDER
TO BE IN A POSITION TO GIVE FIRST-HAND
EVIDENCE OF THESE THINGS IF EVER, IN
THE FUTURE, THERE DEVELOPS A TENDENCY TO
CHARGE THESE ALLEGATIONS TO PROPAGANDA.

GEN. DWIGHT DAVID EISENHOWER
SUPREME COMMANDER OF THE ALLIED FORCES
OHRDRUF CONCENTRATION CAMP
APRIL 15, 1945

102 Walsh-McLean Mansion

A doomed marriage and a cursed diamond

When Evalyn Walsh was 12 years old, her father discovered an actual gold mine, and she became one of the wealthiest teenagers in the country. At 17 years old, she received an incredible gift from her dad: a brand-new mansion on Massachusetts Avenue, then known as Millionaire's Row. The mansion was said to cost $835,000 to construct and another $2 million to furnish and decorate – an unimaginable sum in 1903. It had 60 rooms, a theater, a ballroom, a grand staircase, and a three-deck promenade in the center foyer. It was in this extraordinary setting where Evalyn met Ned.

Edward "Ned" Beale McLean was a scion of a wealthy publishing company, who already had a reputation for copious gambling and drinking. A whirlwind romance led to their elopement in 1908, followed by a lavish honeymoon adventure through Europe and the Middle East. As they traveled, they bought cars, clothing, art, and jewelry, including the 92.5 carat diamond, the Star of the East.

In 1911, they purchased the piece of jewelry that would be linked to their lives forever – the Hope Diamond. The couple purchased the 45.52 carat blue diamond for $180,000 – almost $5 million today. Evalyn adored flaunting the diamond, wearing it constantly, even when just lounging around her mansion. The McLeans threw lavish parties, often spending thousands of dollars in a single night.

But things turned south for the pair. A messy divorce followed, and Ned was deemed legally insane in 1933. Evalyn would spend the second half of her life dealing with her unfaithful husband, the loss of multiple children, and the draining of her financial resources. When she died in 1947, her estate was deeply in debt, partially due to her unfailing generosity with her money. She is entombed today at Rock Creek Cemetery. The mansion retains its splendor.

Address 2020 Massachusetts Avenue, Washington, DC 20036, www.embassyofindonesia.org |
Getting there Metro to Dupont Circle (Red Line); bus N6 to Massachusetts Avenue & 20th
Street NW | Hours Unrestricted to view from outside, tours available by appointment only |
Tip You can see the famous Hope Diamond on display at the National Museum of Natural
History (10th Street & Constitution Avenue NW, www.naturalhistory.si.edu).

103 Wangari Gardens

Dr. Maathai, Nobel Peace Prize Laureate

Her work started in the mountains of Kenya and reached all the way to the Park View neighborhood of Washington, DC. The local garden is named in honor of Dr. Wangari Muta Maathai, an internationally renowned biologist committed to environmental activism, sustainable ecosystems, and community engagement.

The garden was founded by two DC locals. One was a graduate student studying history at George Mason University, and the other was an elementary school teacher who taught food sustainability and managed a local agricultural center. They mobilized members of their neighborhood to take ownership of individual farming plots and collectively cultivated this abandoned land. This holistic approach to urban development aligned with the philosophies of Dr. Maathai who believed that community-based tree planting could increase quality of life.

The Green Belt Movement was founded by Wangari Maathai in 1977 to specifically address the needs of women in rural Kenya, who were facing food insecurity due to the overdevelopment of fertile land. Natural resources like firewood and water had become scarce. Wangari Maathai's solution was to provide a monetary stipend to plant seeds and grow trees. This initiative empowered women economically and created a sustainable ecosystem where the trees planted would provide wood for fire and water for cooking. With access to these resources, community members could eat more nutritious meals, participate in trade, or build infrastructure for shelter or fences.

When Dr. Wangari Maathai became the first African woman to receive the Nobel Peace Prize, the Green Belt movement had successfully planted over 30 million trees. She expressed in her speech a particular mindfulness for women and girls, as well as her belief that sustainable environmentalism is directly linked to democracy, human rights, and economic opportunity.

Address 416 Kenyan Street NW, Washington, DC 20010, +1 (202) 670-5459, wangarigardens.wordpress.com, wangarigardens@gmail.com | Getting there Metro to Columbia Heights (Green and Yellow Line); bus H2 or H4 to Irving Street & Park Place NW | Hours Unrestricted | Tip Visit a tree planted by Representative Barbara Lee in honor of Wangari Maathai on the grounds of the United States Capitol Building (First Street SE, www.aoc.gov/tree).

104_ Warner Theatre

Take a stroll among the sidewalk stars

While Hollywood may boast the most famous Walk of Fame, you may be surprised to discover that outside of the Warner Theatre in the heart of downtown DC, are some brass stars accompanied by famous names in cement. While the sidewalk stars were installed when the theatre was renovated in 2001, the history of the Warner goes back much further.

The theatre was first developed in the early 1920s as a movie palace, presenting live Vaudeville performances alongside silent films. In addition to the theatre, it also boasted a rooftop garden, ballroom, and restaurant. The Earle, as the theatre was called, had its own dance troupe known as the Roxyettes. These young women would perform before and after films, doing precision choreography in unison, much like the more famous Rockettes at Radio City Music Hall. In 1947, the theatre was renamed for producer Harry Warner, and the focus moved exclusively to films. After several reincarnations, it was brought back to its former glory in 1992.

When the grand reopening gala took place, guests were invited to attend in Roaring Twenties attire to commemorate the theatre's founding era. Frank Sinatra and Shirley MacLaine, who took ballet classes from Mary Day of the Washington Ballet Company, performed. Both stars penned their signatures in cement to commemorate the occasion – and a tradition was born. Other performers would pass through the theatre to perform and sign their names in cement blocks that were stored away. The cement pavers were kept in storage until 2001, when they were set in the sidewalk. There are over 40 stars recognized today, including notable female performers like Mary Day, Liza Minnelli, Sweet Honey in the Rock, Paula Abdul, Morgan Fairchild and Bonnie Raitt, who included the phrase "no nukes" with her signature. One can never truly escape politics in Washington, DC, even at the theatre.

Address 513 13th Street NW, Washington, DC 20004, +1 (202) 783-4000, www.warnertheatredc.com | Getting there Metro to Metro Center (Blue, Orange, Red, and Silver Line); bus D6 to E & 13th Streets NW | Hours See website for schedule | Tip Coretta Scott King presided over the ceremony to bury a time capsule of items pertaining to her husband Dr. Martin Luther King Jr. in nearby Freedom Plaza in 1988 (1455 Pennsylvania Avenue NW, www.downtowndc.org/go/freedom-plaza).

105 — Washington Mystics
Watch women win at basketball

Local sports fans celebrated two team championships in October of 2019, but only one team paraded down historic Pennsylvania Avenue. The men from the Washington Nationals baseball team celebrated their Major League Baseball (MLB) World Series win in first-class style, riding on top of floats while being cheered on by fans along the route headed toward the United States Capitol Building. But while top male athletes were rising to the height of their careers, the female athletes from the Washington Mystics had to forego their Women's National Basketball Association (WNBA) championship parade.

Following the WNBA finals, several players immediately hopped on planes, including Most Valuable Player Emma Meesseman, to head overseas and play with their secondary teams. These professional athletes earn supplemental income from the international leagues, as the average salary for a WNBA player in 2019 was just $75,000 per year, seven times less than their male counterparts. The team did eventually collaborate with city officials to host a parade seven months later, only to have it cancelled due to the global pandemic.

Despite the disparities in equal opportunities, the Washington Mystics continue to bring talent and energy to the Entertainment & Sports Arena. After calling the Verizon Center home, the Mystics moved to southeast DC and kicked-off the inaugural 2019 season at their new court with a championship victory, the first in franchise history since it was established in 1998. The team seeded first, bypassed two rounds of the playoffs, and finished with a season record of 26-8, taking the majority of a final five-game series against the Connecticut Sun. In a venue that hosts 4,200 fans, every seat is sure to feel like you are courtside. With the thrill of the game and the talent of the home team, you won't want to miss any WNBA games in DC.

Address 1100 Oak Drive SE, Washington, DC 20032, www.esaontherise.com/washington-mystics | Getting there Metro to Congress Heights (Green Line); bus A2, A8 to Martin Luther King Avenue SE & 5th Street SE | Hours See website for schedule | Tip The surrounding historic district was Saint Elizabeths Hospital, a building complex that housed the nation's first government-funded mental health hospital, established primarily through efforts by social reformer Dorothea Dix (1100 Alabama Avenue SE, www.nps.gov/places/st-elizabeths-hospital.htm).

106__Washington Spirit

Professional soccer scores in the nation's capital

Women's soccer is one of the fastest growing sports in the US. From youth leagues to the professionals, the game is rooted deep in modern American culture. There are two events in history that fueled the momentum for its popularity: Title IX and the 1999 World Cup.

Title IX of the Education Amendments Act of 1972 was a federal law that prohibited sex discrimination under any federally funded education program, essentially mandating equal access to sports in schools. Prior to Title IX, only 700 female athletes were playing high school soccer. Participation rates under the law have increased 1,000 percent since then, as generations of girls have now benefited from this policy authored by Congresswoman Patsy Mink. And 40 million people saw its impact during the 1999 FIFA Women's World Cup Final.

The United States won in the final goal of the penalty shoot-out with the Chinese National Team. Women's soccer was the topic of international conversation, and Team USA was at the fore. Fast forward to the 2019 National Team, who made headlines as World Cup champions and equal pay advocates. But before these championship players stepped into the spotlight, many of them got their start here in the nation's capital.

The first professional soccer team in DC was the Washington Freedom, which was formed in 2001 and played at RFK Stadium in the WUSA league. The roster included Mia Hamm as a founding player, and Abby Wambach was recruited for the second season. The current National Women's Soccer League (NWSL) emerged in 2012, and the Washington Spirit competed in the league's inaugural season with star players Ashlyn Harris and Ali Krieger on the roster. Team investors include two first daughters, Chelsea Clinton and Jenna Bush Hager, and two Olympic gold medalists, Dominique Dawes and Briana Scurry. The nation's capital remains a city of opportunity for women's athletics.

Address 100 Potomac Avenue SW, Washington, DC 20024, +1 (202) 587-5000, www.washingtonspirit.com, fans@washspirit.com | **Getting there** Metro to Waterfront (Green Line); bus 74 to 2nd & R Streets SW | **Hours** See website for schedule | **Tip** If you're looking to get into the athletic spirit yourself, join a social sports league with DC Fray. The group plans recreational league play, events, and more, all centered around the ethos to make fun possible (www.dcfray.com).

107 The Whittemore House

She was a secretary… in the Presidential Cabinet

If the Whittemore House could speak, its voice would echo generations of women who have gathered within these historic walls. As feminists have battled to ascend the mountain of national politics, the most progressive women in government have embraced this unique space to harness their message, build powerful coalitions, and record their histories.

Since 1927, this mansion has been home to the Women's National Democratic Club, an organization that emerged from the ratification of the 19th Amendment by co-founders Emily Newell Blair and Mrs. J. Bordon "Daisy" Harriman. The mansion was originally built in the 1890s for opera singer Sarah Adams Whittemore and mindfully designed to elevate her musical performances. The building is known to have exceptional acoustics, which is perhaps why Eleanor Roosevelt (see ch. 23) decided to hold a series of all-women press conferences in the upstairs library, now named in her honor. Complementing the book collection is a wooden desk that once belonged to Frances Perkins, the first woman to serve in a Presidential cabinet. As Secretary of Labor under FDR, she built the foundation of modern policies like Social Security, a minimum wage, and the 40-hour work week; she helped the country recover from the Great Depression and see promise in the New Deal. Perkins specifically prioritized protection for women and children, having personally witnessed the infamous Triangle Shirtwaist Factory Fire.

The legacy of liberal women is preserved in the Women's National Democratic Club. In 1973, the same year that Roe v. Wade was decided, this DuPont Circle building was entered into the National Register of Historical Places. The Whittemore House is not only an event space, but also a museum where visitors can admire a statue of Bella Abzug, a portrait of Marjorie Merriweather Post (see ch. 42), or a photo of Eleanor Holmes Norton (see ch. 20).

Address 1526 New Hampshire Avenue, Washington, DC 20036, +1 (240) 343-5190, www.thewhittemorehouse.com | Getting there Metro to Dupont Circle (Red Line); bus G2 to P & 18th Streets NW | Hours Daily by appointment only | Tip Visit the National League of American Pen Women, founded because women journalists were barred from joining associated organizations, for a rich array of public events (1300 17th Street NW, www.nlapw.org).

108 The Willard Hotel

Home to peacocks, poets, and first ladies

The Willard Intercontinental Washington, DC is one of the oldest hotels in the city, hosting an impressive roster of notable names and famous faces over the past two centuries. When downtown DC was dominated by male-only spaces, the hotel offered areas designated for women, including a Ladies Lounge, a private entrance for ladies to enter and exit the hotel, and the aptly named Peacock Alley, which you can still visit off the main lobby. Modeled after a similar space in New York's Waldorf-Astoria, the alley was designed for showcasing one's latest fashions, much like a peacock. More scandalous than the clothing was the Pompeian Room, where men and women commingled socially, and women were even permitted to smoke.

The Willard Hotel was home to two first ladies: Grace Coolidge and Florence Harding. Coolidge lived here with her husband Calvin from 1921–1923 while he was vice president. As second lady, she volunteered for the Red Cross (see ch. 90) and solidified her reputation as one of the most popular women in the city, hosting and entertaining in her unpretentious yet elegant style.

After Florence Harding's husband died in office, she left Washington, DC. But she returned to rent a suite at the hotel in 1924. Harding had been the force behind her husband's political career, and she intended to work as hard in securing his legacy as she had in making him president. Sadly, she left after a few months due to poor health. She perished later that year.

One of the most notable women to stay at the Willard was Julia Ward Howe, poet, abolitionist, and suffragist. In November 1861, she awoke around dawn with lyrics in her head. She had recently attended a review of Union troops and was moved by soldiers singing "John Brown's Body." She set pen to paper and wrote new words to the song's tune, sent a copy to the editor of the Atlantic Monthly, and the "Battle Hymn of the Republic" was born.

Address 1401 Pennsylvania Avenue NW, Washington, DC 20004, +1 (202) 628-9100, www.washington.intercontinental.com | Getting there Metro to Metro Center (Blue, Orange, Red, and Silver Line); bus 230, 250 to 14th Street & Pennsylvania Avenue NW | Hours Lobby unrestricted | Tip Riggs Washington DC, located in the historic Riggs National Bank building, is an upscale hotel with four suites inspired by four lesser-known first ladies: Ida McKinley, Caroline Harrison, Louisa Adams, and Angelica Van Buren (900 F Street NW, www.riggsdc.com).

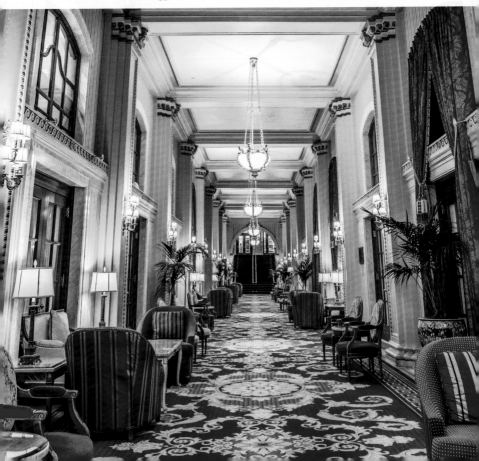

109 *Women in Politics* Mural

Equality is on the ballot

With nearly 15 murals in DC, the work of artist Lisa Marie Thalhammer can be recognized by her use of bright colors, playful images, and symbolic messages. Taking a photo in front of her rainbow *LOVE* mural in Blagden Alley has become a bucket-list item for tourists, while her series of DC Statehood murals sends locals on a scavenger hunt. One of her most powerful pieces of art however, rises subtly above the skyline of the U Street Corridor.

Lisa Marie's mural *Women in Politics* puts feminism on full display. Washingtonians are quick to express their political convictions, but this thought-provoking image poses more questions than it does answers. It's art that requires contemplation, and what better way to do that than with a mimosa over brunch? Though *Women in Politics* is visible from the sidewalk below, the best view is from the rooftop deck of neighborhood restaurant Local 16, whose owner Aman Ayoubi commissioned the artwork.

It's a mural that exposes a new element each time it's viewed, like Madam Elephant dressed in a blue women's suit outfit or Ms. Donkey wearing her fire engine red high heels. The admirer is challenged to determine whether the women are arm wrestling in opposition or giving a supportive high five to each other. Historically, there is precedent for both scenarios.

An overlooked partisan match-up in 1956 featured Democrat Eleanor Roosevelt (see ch. 23) and Republican Margaret Chase Smith. They were the first people to participate in a Presidential debate on television when the male candidates nominated them both as spokeswomen. A different example showcases women's bipartisanship led by Senator Barbara Mikulski. Her proposed "Zone of Civility" included regular dinner gatherings for Senate women to build personal respect for one another. They would ultimately be credited for their collaborative leadership in ending the 2013 government shutdown.

Address 1602 U Street NW, Washington, DC 20009, +1 (202) 265-2828, www.localsixteen.com, info@localsixteen.com | Getting there Metro to U Street (Yellow and Green Line); bus S9 to U & 16th Streets NW | Hours Unrestricted | Tip As part of the project #MuralsDC51, Lisa Marie Thalhammer painted a mural portrait of the District's Congresswoman Eleanor Holmes Norton, whose career has been widely focused on securing statehood for Washington, DC (4608 14th Street NW, www.lisamariestudio.com).

110 Woodrow Wilson House
Home to America's first female president

Edith Bolling Galt was a widow in her forties when she was introduced to the newly widowed president, Woodrow Wilson, in March 1915. Despite being more than 15 years her senior, Wilson took an immediate interest in her and proposed just weeks after their meeting. The couple wed in December 1915.

Edith Wilson served as First Lady during WWI. Leading by example, she observed meatless Mondays and wheatless Wednesdays to bolster the rationing effort. She hired sheep to graze on the White House lawn and auctioned their wool for the war effort. She knitted trench helmets and sewed pajamas for the troops, and she volunteered with the Red Cross (see ch. 90) at Union Station.

In October 1919, Woodrow Wilson suffered a massive stroke that left him unable to perform the duties of office. To protect her husband and his legacy, Edith chose to conceal the truth of Wilson's health from his cabinet and the press, believing they would force him to resign, which would only further his debilitation. While Edith wrote in her 1939 memoirs that she "never made a single decision regarding the disposition of public affairs," she was, in essence, the eyes and ears of the American presidency for six months. She determined who was allowed in the White House and what papers Wilson would see, and she relayed his decisions to government officials.

When Wilson's presidency ended, the couple moved into this mansion on S Street, which Wilson bought as a wedding gift for Edith, sight unseen. He would only live there for a short time before dying in 1924. Edith remained there until her death in 1961 and bequeathed the home and all of its original furnishings to the National Trust for Historic Preservation. The house looks as much as possible as it did in 1924. Edith maintained their personal library, the piano the Wilsons had in the White House, and the many treasured gifts from foreign dignitaries.

Address 2340 S Street NW, Washington, DC 20008, +1 (202) 387-4062, www.woodrowwilsonhouse.org, wilsonhouse@woodrowwilsonhouse.org | Getting there Bus N6 to Massachusetts Avenue & S Street NW | Hours See website | Tip Woodrow and Edith Wilson are the only President and First Lady to be laid to rest in the District of Columbia. The couple are buried together at Washington National Cathedral in the Wilson Tomb (3101 Wisconsin Avenue NW, www.cathedral.org).

111 Zitkala-Ša, aka Red Bird
Women's Suffrage Mural: Zitkala-Ša, a Native voice

Thaté Iyóhiwi was a loving mother who wanted to provide her daughter with the best educationpossible. But opportunity did not come without sacrifice on the Yankton Indian Reservation in South Dakota. For her daughter Zitkala-Ša, or Red Bird, to broaden her perspective beyond the West, she would have to leave her native culture behind and accompany the missionaries to the East.

Thaté's "mother's intuition" was to resist the idea of being separated from her daughter, but she rationalized her final approval. "The palefaces, who owe us a large debt for stolen lands, have begun to pay a tardy injustice in offering some education to our children. But I know my daughter must suffer keenly in this experiment." It was 1884, and the missionaries promised Zitkala-Ša an abundance of fresh fruit and an experience riding on a modern train, which she called an "iron horse." She and seven other children set out for "The Land of Red Apples," arriving at the Quaker school in Wabash, Indiana, where she would drop her native identity as Red Bird and take the name Gertrude Simmons.

Over time, she became keenly aware of the intense emphasis on assimilation the program forced onto Native children. In her book *American Indian Stories*, Simmons would write, "I slowly comprehended that the large army of white teachers in Indian schools had a larger missionary creed than I had suspected. It was one which included self-preservation quite as much as Indian education." She claimed to have lost her connection to nature and vowed to spend her energies "working for the Indian race."

Zitkala-Ša became one of the most accomplished advocates for the representation of Native Americans and women. The cover of her original 1921 book matches the pattern behind MISS CHELOVE's portrait mural. Visitors can also pay respects at Arlington National Cemetery where she is buried with her husband.

Address 2027 Martin Luther King Avenue SE, Washington, DC 20020, www.chelove.com | Getting there Metro to Anacostia (Green); bus P6 to Martin Luther King Avenue & U Street SE | Hours Unrestricted | Tip Frederick Douglas established Cedar Hill, his home in Anacostia, in 1877 and used it as a base of operations for his work, including his fight for women's suffrage (1411 W Street SE, www.nps.gov/frdo/index.htm).

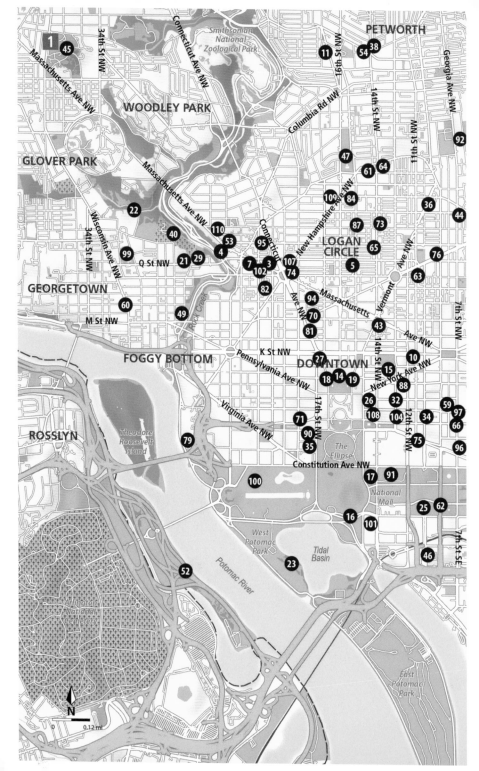

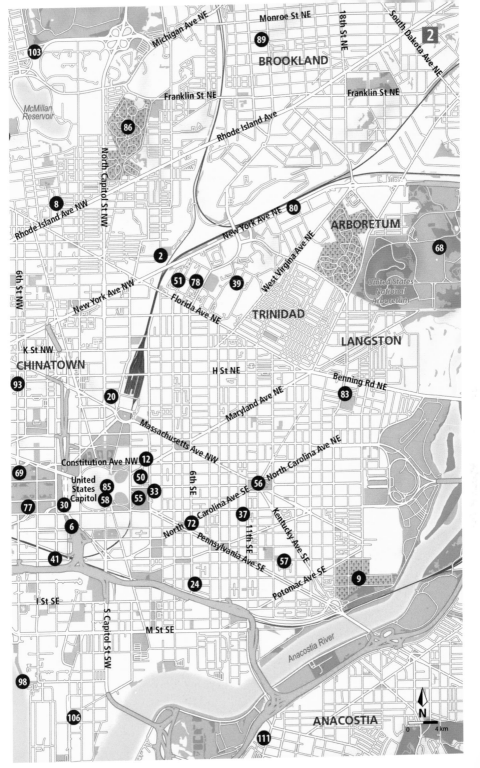

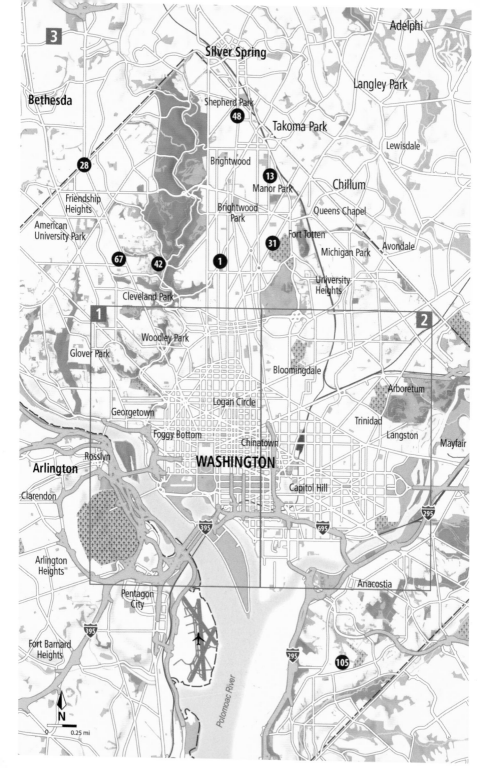

Andréa Seiger, John Dean
111 Places in Washington
That You Must Not Miss
ISBN 978-3-7408-0258-5

Allison Robicelli, John Dean
111 Places in Baltimore
That You Must Not Miss
ISBN 978-3-7408-0158-8

Heather Kapplow, Kim Windyka,
Alyssa Wood
111 Places in Boston
That You Must Not Miss
ISBN 978-3-7408-1558-5

Jo-Anne Elikann
111 Places in New York
That You Must Not Miss
ISBN 978-3-95451-052-8

Amy Bizzarri, Susie Inverso
111 Places in Chicago
That You Must Not Miss
ISBN 978-3-7408-1030-6

Laurel Moglen, Julia Posey,
Lyudmila Zotova
111 Places in Los Angeles
That You Must Not Miss
ISBN 978-3-7408-0906-5

Floriana Petersen, Steve Werney
111 Places in San Francisco
That You Must Not Miss
ISBN 978-3-95451-609-4

Cristyle Egitto, Jakob Takos
111 Places in Palm Beach
That You Must Not Miss
ISBN 978-3-7408-0897-6

Dana DuTerroil, Joni Fincham,
Daniel Jackson
111 Places in Houston
That You Must Not Miss
ISBN 978-3-7408-0896-9

Flora Molton (ch. 32): Cast Bronze, Paint & Stainless Steel, 2019, Charles Bergen Studios, funded by the DC Commission on the Arts and Humanities Public Art Program and the Downtown DC Business Improvement District

Founders Memorial (ch. 35): Gertrude Vanderbilt Whitney, sculptor

Thomas Hopkins Gallaudet and Alice Cogswell (ch. 39): Daniel Chester French, sculptor

Ruth Bader Ginsburg Mural (ch. 43): Andrea Sheehan and Julie Coyle

Joan of Arc (ch. 47): Paul Dubois, sculptor

Mary McLeod Bethune (ch. 56): Robert Berks, sculptor

Portrait of Belva Lockwood with Jokes the Parrot (ch. 57): Leslie Holt, artist, 2019

Lucretia Coffin Mott (ch. 59): Joseph Kyle, 1842; National Portrait Gallery, Smithsonian Institute; gift of Mrs. Alan Valentine

The Loge (ch. 69): Mary Cassatt, Chester Dale Collection; courtesy National Gallery of Art, Washington

Nuns of the Battlefield (ch. 70): Jerome Connor

Olive Risley Seward (ch. 72): John Cavanaugh, sculptor

The Courage Within Me (ch. 79): Michelle Angela Ortiz; 2019, acrylic paintings reproduced on plastic panels; in collaboration with: Anacostia High School students with teaching artist, Cheryl Foster, and teacher, Jeria Carter; Columbia Heights Educational Campus students with teaching artist, Shaunte Gates and teacher, Mandy McCullough; Dunbar High School students with teaching artist, Sera Boeno, and teacher, Zachary Jackson; Eastern High School students with teaching artist, Preston Sampson, and teacher, Zalika Perkins

RBG Tribute Mural (ch. 84): Rose Jaffe

Sakakawea (ch. 85): Leonard Crunelle, sculptor

Sheep by the Sea (ch. 88): Rosa Bonheur, 1865; Oil on cradled panel, 12 3/4 x 18 in.; National Museum of Women in the Arts, Gift of Wallace and Wilhelmina Holladay

Titanic Memorial (ch. 98): Gertrude Vanderbilt Whitney, sculptor

Vietnam Women's Memorial (ch. 100): © 1993 Vietnam Women's Memorial Foundation Inc. Glenna Goodacre, Sculptor

Women in Politics Mural (ch. 109):
Lisa Marie Thalhammer @lisamariestudio

Legacy of Resilience (ch. 111): (L-R) *"Onward and Upward We Go"*, 2020, Candice Taylor; *"Ain't I A Woman"*, 2020, Mia DuVall; *"Lifting as we Climb"*, 2020, MISSCHELOVE.

Funded by the DC Commission on the Arts and Humanities and in partnership with DC Department of Public Works

I am grateful to Becca, Cindy, and the TOHO team for rallying around big ideas with me. For our colleagues in tourism and TOHO supporters for believing in this vision early on; for everyone who contributed along the way and for all who are joining our journey now. To Karen and Andrea for providing guidance and encouragement within the 111 community. For my parents and family who keep me grounded – and to my closest friends for their unconditional love and acceptance. Thank you.

Kaitlin Calogera

It would be impossible to truly express our gratitude to the passionate people at every site who made this book possible. Thank you to our amazing colleagues in D.C.'s tourism industry, especially at A Tour of Her Own and DC By Foot. Special thanks to Tawnya Azar, Erin Blasco, Jamie Burchfield, Dr. Arlene Kelly and Tawny Holmes Esq., Robert Pohl, Nanci Visser, and Brett Zonker for assistance above and beyond. Deepest appreciation to the team at Emons and my incredible partners-in-crime, Kait and Cindy. I could not have done this – or anything else – without Matt, Mom, and Katie.

Rebecca Grawl

I am fortunate to have met these two amazing peers Kait and Rebecca to steer alongside as this project could not have been possible without them. My sincerest appreciation for the many private tours and laughter cherished during this process. I also want to express the gratitude, support, and encouragement of my loving Husband Adam. Thank you for always being by my side and giving me the freedom to dream. Thanks to my parents Arlene Schiavetto Staliunas and Amadeu Staliunas for always believing in me and allowing me to find my path. Lastly, I dedicate this book to one more amazing woman, Antonia da Silva Leme Schiavetto, in loving memory, Vovózinha do meu coração!

Cynthia Schiavetto Staliunas

Kaitlin Calogera embarked on a journey of entrepreneurship when she launched A Tour Of Her Own, the first tourism company in Washington, DC to focus exclusively on women's history. As a licensed tour guide, she recognized a lack of women's stories being represented in public spaces so she mobilized her community to reframe the traditional narrative through special events and historical tours. With a degree in History and a background coaching women's athletics, Kaitlin believes in the power of tourism to promote gender equality and education beyond the classroom.

Rebecca Grawl is a professional DC tour guide with more than a decade's experience in public history, museum education, and tourism and is particularly proud of her involvement as a founding member of A Tour of Her Own, the first tour company in DC to focus exclusively on women's history. She is a proud graduate of Randolph-Macon Woman's College, member of the National Society Daughters of the American Revolution as well as an alumnae and senior leader with the National Society Children of the American Revolution. Rebecca has been featured on *Mysteries at the Museum* on the Travel Channel, *Tour Guide Tell All* podcast, and in local press outlets such as WAMU/DCist, *Washingtonian, Washington City Paper,* and more.

Cynthia Schiavetto Staliunas is an internationally awarded and published fine art and destination photographer based in the Washington, DC area. With a background in psychology and cosmetology, her mission is to revolutionize the way women see themselves through her photography, with a focus on and passion for phototherapy and women's empowerment. She enjoys traveling the world and learning new languages. www.schiavettophotography.com